THE HEART OF THE TEAM

LIFE LESSONS ON AND OFF THE COURT

BILL RESLER

Coach of the Roosevelt Roughriders
and star of The Heart of the Game

WITH CASEY McNERTHNEY

SASQUATCH BOOKS
SEATTLE

For Davico

Printed in the United States of America
Published by Sasquatch Books
Distributed by Publishers Group West
16 15 14 13 12 11 10 09 08 07 06   9 8 7 6 5 4 3 2 1

Cover photographs: David Belisle (top) and Bob Suh (bottom)
Cover design: Bob Suh
Interior design: Stewart A. Williams
Interior composition: Elizabeth Cromwell
Interior photographs:
        Page 2: Courtesy of Bill Resler
        Page 106: Courtesy Gilbert W. Arias/*Seattle Post-Intelligencer*
        Page 150: Courtesy of Lindsey Wilson
        All other photographs by Casey McNerthney

Library of Congress Cataloging-in-Publication Data is available.
ISBN 1-57061-518-7

Sasquatch Books
119 South Main Street, Suite 400
Seattle, WA 98104
(206) 467-4300
www.sasquatchbooks.com
custserv@sasquatchbooks.com

Contents

Foreword

Normally, during basketball games, coaches are passionate about the level of play and the elements of the game itself, and their enthusiasm for the sport extends to the players around them. With Bill Resler, the first thing you notice is his passion for the players, regardless of whether he's coaching in the state championship or in an after-practice pickup game. It's obvious to me that he cares for his players as if they were his own daughters. This is what enables him to get the most out of them on the court and in life.

I've had much success throughout my basketball career, but to be honest, most of the life lessons I learned through basketball I learned in high school.

To me, high school basketball is where you develop habits that will stay with you for the rest of your life and career—things as simple as how to make a correct bounce pass and as complex as how to deal with the mental aspects of a high-pressure situation. Many of those same lessons are conveyed here by Coach Resler in an intriguing style that makes you feel like you're a part of Roosevelt's Inner Circle.

High school basketball is where essential characteristics such as discipline, loyalty, determination, and accountability are first learned, and the habits you form on the court stay with you forever.

I like Coach Resler's style because he understands that while his teenage players might not fully understand his lessons when they're in high school, they will call on those lessons decades from now in their professional careers and as parents and spouses.

In this book, Coach Resler shows the value of lessons such as "never give up," "work hard, play hard," and "no championship without sacrifice." These lessons are extremely important in basketball, but even more so in life. The expectations Coach Resler has of his players are terrific. He doesn't allow them to be selfish and he puts them in an environment where they can succeed and flourish. Of course, this doesn't always come easy, and sometimes he has to demonstrate "tough love" with players and parents. Coach Resler knows when it's time to work and when it's time to play and that it's important to distinguish between the two. Because he's taken his own lessons to heart, he can help his players to grow as athletes and as young adults.

I was fortunate to be part of a state championship team in high school. Winning was fun, but it was the friendships, bonds, sisterly arguments, life lessons, and everything in between that made the experience enjoyable. Coach Resler understands that having fun and building those teammate bonds are more important than any final score. That's what impresses me, and that is what has made him a successful teacher.

In my opinion, there is no greater way to learn about life than by playing sports. Through basketball, I have learned what it means to work hard. I recall the lessons I learned on the court and use them for the challenges I face off the court. I'm confident that Coach Resler's players will benefit from his teachings for the rest of their lives. And I hope this book will give you the same kind of strength Coach Resler has given—and continues to give—each and every one of his players.

—Sue Bird, October 2006

Introduction

In the spring of 1998, I interviewed to be head coach of the Roosevelt High School girls basketball team. The first question the nine-person interview committee asked was, "What's your coaching philosophy?"

I told them that during games, I want my players to have more fun than the opponents while being focused on their goals. Over the course of a season, I want them to learn the value of hard work and understand that whatever they put into life is what they'll get out of it. Life is not about winning and losing, it's about improving yourself inch by inch, I said.

I talked about giving the girls power, instilling aggression, devoting attention to even the least-skilled player. I said that teaching life lessons was much more important than having an undefeated season. A few days after the interview, I was hired.

Early in my first season, I met documentary director Ward Serrill, and when he came to a Roughrider game, he was astonished by the aggressive determination of our athletes. He immediately understood the lessons I was trying to encourage. For seven years, he filmed the various Roosevelt teams for what became the film *The Heart of the Game*, which was released nationwide in June 2006.

I was reminded each time I saw the documentary in a theater that the film provided more than two dozen laugh-out-loud moments, but most of those laughs were at my oddball personality. Fans of the film have asked me why I tell my players they're wolves, why I say they should sink their teeth into their opponents' necks and draw blood. They want to know how I helped once-reticent Roosevelt girls become players who knew they would not win every game but would win every hypothetical fistfight that occurred. People have asked how I took my team to the state tournament as a no-name, first-year coach and eventually earned the best overall win-loss record in what many coaches consider Washington's most difficult league. And almost all the conversations lead to this pivotal question: "Have you ever thought about writing a book?"

Many years ago, a colleague at the University of Washington gave me a tape recorder and told me to cut loose. Put your stories on tape, he said, and when your tapes are full, turn the material into a book. I thanked him for the recorder and the encouragement, though I never thought people would care about stories told by an oddball liberal who loves tax law and high school basketball.

But when people wanted to know more, it made me think a lot about what is truly important, and I started drafting this book. Because time restrictions prevented the documentary from focusing on multiple players, some of the most moving situations I've witnessed are only briefly mentioned, if at all. Writing the remarkable stories of players I've coached, some who were stars of *The Heart of the Game* and some who were barely noticed in the film, has allowed me to flesh out their fullness with all the flavor of their character.

Unfortunately, many students find school tedious. Educators have a duty to find a way to engage teenagers in learning, and basketball is one thing I am passionate about. I am lucky enough to teach tax at the University of Washington, which I love to do and view as my calling. However, at Roosevelt, the classroom I was issued was the basketball court. So instead of teaching with books and a chalkboard,

I try to infuse the athletes with life lessons between heart-pounding-tough, fundamental basketball drills. The sole reason I coach is that I believe my life lessons should be learned by teenagers.

The basic description of basketball makes it seem ridiculous: one team is trying to put a ball through a hoop and the other is trying to prevent it. Really, the game alone has no worthwhile purpose whatsoever. But teaching how the game is played can show players that if they work as a group, they can accomplish things despite another group trying to prevent those accomplishments. It teaches girls to own their turf while playing in a team setting. I believe basketball is a perfect platform to teach lessons for life.

Each year, my teams have themes, such as "Pack of Wolves" or "Pride of Lions," used to teach all-out aggression and help girls live in the moment. The themes are meant to separate them from their crazy, teenage jitters and allow them to take control of their environment, go completely wild, and have total fun without regard for what the rest of the world thinks. The themes are a gimmick to help the girls be themselves, and the life lessons will become a part of the girls—not always when they're 17, but maybe when they're 30.

I teach my players that having fun is most important. A concept I live by is that you should try to fashion each day to be better than yesterday. I tell players that when they accidentally hurt people, which is inevitable in life, they must fix their mistakes by helping those wronged work through their disappointment. Try to be perfect, I say, though keep in mind perfection is impossible because everyone makes mistakes.

Like most people, I have my share of imperfections. I certainly do not consider myself a candidate for sainthood. And in this book, I do not offer my past as a model way of living. Many people are sure to disagree with personal decisions I have made. I believe that you should not be judged by the mistakes you've made in life but rather should be judged by how you fix them. Some parents have questioned my two previous marriages, both of which ended in divorce. These things happen in life, but what's important is the incredible respect I have for my ex-wives and the strong relationships I maintain with my daughters.

Because my life contains peccadilloes that are common to humanity, I feel my life lessons are more realistic. We learn through our mistakes, and it is our job as adults to share the lessons we've painfully learned through experience in a positive and instructive way. I very much doubt that I am through making mistakes, but I still aim to make each day perfect despite the fact that perfection hasn't happened yet.

I could talk for days about my theories and experiences, but I'm nowhere near as compelling as the players I have coached. They're the reason our teams have done well. They're the ones who make the seasons memorable. And that's why my essential life lessons are taught in this book through them—teenagers whose experiences demonstrate these lessons far better than I could ever explain them.

The first chapter tells the lessons I learned in my own life, and my recollections of how I understood them. The lessons were not learned as much in the classroom as they were through raw experience. More important than my successes, I explain some mistakes I made and the loving family that helped me realize those mistakes were part of the learning process.

My life is a collection of stories, and usually when I deal with some sort of human interaction, I try to find the humor in the situation. To me, life is a series of problems. I don't mean this normatively; instead, I see problems as solutions about to happen. As I encounter events in my life, I can nearly always tease the whimsy out of situations that are often cloaked by the actions of those involved. The first chapter allows you, the reader, to observe my approach to life and also learn a little about how this method was given to me by my family.

The first chapter shows that much of my approach is a result of living in a family where humor was a major part of the experience. It was not so much that my parents instructed me; rather, they allowed me to take in my own lessons as I lived my life in their environment. This led to my similar teaching style. I attempt to create an environment where the student is forced to garner the information themselves. My role is to be the catalyst that promotes hard work while maintaining interest by emphasizing an enjoyable approach to life.

When I was in high school, I didn't have enough life experience to put things in context, which I believe is true for all teenagers. Eventually, teenagers feel they have answers for everything and can't stand to be around their "stupid" parents who have no idea what it's like to be in high school. Parents know their teenage kids are not in control of their life, but the teens think they are, and I feel it's crucial to give them power. That idea is what led to my concept of the Inner Circle, which I feel is a catalyst for the life lessons presented in the rest of the book.

The Roosevelt team consists of the varsity players, junior varsity players, and freshman team, called the JVC. Players and friends are part of the team, as are coaches and fans that follow the Roughriders' progress. But the real team is the Inner Circle, comprising varsity athletes who govern the team administratively and psychologically.

The Inner Circle doesn't make life or death decisions or make rulings with a major global impact—they're deciding what tomorrow's practice will be like, or whether the team should have captains. Their belief that the decision is important makes it so. The Inner Circle and the choices teenagers make among a mass of opinions help players grasp what I teach.

These essential life lessons are described in the following chapters through the experiences of specific players. Each is interesting, humorous, and at times may make you reach for a tissue. Through the unpredictable experiences of these girls, they (and I) have learned how to be better people. Some stories tell of state tournament games and unforgettable league championships. Other chapters tell of girls who didn't help us win with their point contributions, but did help us win with their unrelenting, breathtaking spirit.

I believe winning is a state of mind, not a result. If you scored more points than the opponent, it doesn't necessarily mean you won the game; it only means that you scored more points. Reporters and fans are not invited into the inner sanctum of the locker room to find out what dynamics made the difference in a game. They rarely see that wins on the court aren't nearly as moving as watching girls learn lessons they'll utilize for the rest of their lives.

High school basketball games last for only 32 minutes. Life, if you're lucky, lasts for decades. Which game do you want to win?

CHAPTER ONE

Who Am I?

TOP: *My mother, Cora Jean Resler, and me, May 1966; BOTTOM: My father, Joseph Howard Resler, and me at Fort Lewis, 1969 (Both photographs courtesy Bill Resler)*

My Introduction to
Life Lessons

I can barely remember the night Ward Serrill first came to watch the Roosevelt Roughriders play their anything-goes, all-out aggression style of basketball. What I do remember is how stunned I was by the post-game statement Ward made after he climbed down from the stands to shake my hand.

"Bill," he said, "I want to film the way you coach."

I'd been introduced to Ward a couple days earlier by Steve Rice, a fellow tax professor at the University of Washington, who'd trained Ward as a CPA. Once Ward had recovered from that experience, he launched a documentary film production company. I was a nobody in the world of high school coaching when Ward and I first met. At the time, Roosevelt was predicted to finish fourth in our five-team division, and the press rarely took notice of our games. In those days, even the WNBA had trouble getting noticed, let alone filling the stands. So I was stunned when Ward told me he wanted to make a documentary about the team and my unconventional coaching methods. Why did he want to waste film on me?

With seven years of filming and editing behind us, even with *The Heart of the Game* wrapped up and distributed, Ward's proposition still seems questionable. More times than I can remember during the process, Ward reiterated it was my on- and off-court teaching methods that compelled him to make the movie—which was no easy feat. Ward dedicated seven years of his life to filming my teams, an ordeal that found Ward fighting almost certain bankruptcy and teeter-tottering on the brink of six near–nervous breakdowns.

When it comes to my coaching style, my main objective is to empower my young players. I want them to have fun while playing with animalistic intensity. I want them to understand the importance of being part of a team, and to know that people judge them not by their mistakes but by how they correct their mistakes. I want them to never give up. Most important, I want them to have fun.

I like basketball, but I'm not there only for the game. Winning is fun, but I couldn't really care less if we lose. I would much prefer to lose by one or two than win by 40. I'm there to teach life lessons, and I believe that the lessons the players learn now will make them exquisite people when they're adults. To be a coach is to say, "I think my life lessons are so valuable, they should be taught to teenagers." To teach them well, a coach must have extreme self-confidence. If you aren't teaching life lessons along with the basketball drills, you shouldn't be a high school coach.

It would be easy to tell you that I project incredible words of wisdom because of a natural brilliance and a life devoid of dull moments. But that would be a lie. In my 60-plus years, I've been fortunate to encounter incredible people who have taught me the essential lessons I now teach my players. All the lessons I teach, especially the most important ones discussed in detail in this book, are rooted to my own life experiences. All I hope is that my life lessons and values rub off on my players, just as I absorbed the lessons I learned from my parents, teachers, and coaches.

My parents played major roles in molding my life philosophies. As an example, I remember one particular teenage evening, when calamitous embarrassment filled my heart and soul as I awaited my dad's arrival to pick me up from work. The year was 1961 and I was a high school sophomore. My first job was bagging groceries at a south Seattle store near my house, and though I didn't enjoy it, I had absolutely no plans to get fired. Though I desperately needed the ride home, part of me hoped my dad wouldn't arrive. I was a vessel carrying only bad news and every fiber in my body was fighting against telling my father what had happened that day.

At the end of that five-hour, Wednesday-evening shift, my manager called me in his office and fired me. He didn't give me examples of what I'd done wrong, though I'm sure he was thinking of the day I put a customer's groceries in her car trunk and laid the bag on its side, causing the contents to saturate the trunk lining on the drive home. And then, of course, there was the day I put two milk cartons flat on the bottom of a bag and stacked groceries on top, causing them to explode—and the customer was the manager's wife. Perhaps on his mind could have been the day I checked in on the punch clock using his card instead of mine. Actually, in the fleeting time it took him to deliver the terrible news, I was unable to recall all of the stupid teenage mistakes I'd made in the few months I had worked there. For him, this was merely a business deal. For me at that age, it was life and death.

No kid wants to bring negative news home to their parents, and with my 16-year-old perspective I thought my parents might never forget my stupid grocery-boy mistakes. Of course, I also worried they'd get really mad at me. I nervously waited for my father and soon enough, here came my family's Buick Invicta rounding the corner and heading my way. It was too late to run and there was no place to hide. Damn! I'd have to face the music.

Seeing my dad's face, he was in a great mood and, alas, it was going to be my responsibility to ruin all of that. I climbed in the Buick, chose to do the brave thing, and, of course, said nothing. I couldn't speak because I knew what I would have to say. I just couldn't do it.

After a few blocks, my dad broke the silence. "What's wrong, Bill?" he injected. At first, I stuck to my guns and said nothing. Then, I gave in. "I got fired," I said. "What for?" he asked. "He told me I had a lack of foresight."

My dad was silent for a couple blocks. What unspoken mystery was he pondering? How long would I be grounded? How would he tell Mom? How much abuse was I going to take from my older sister? Did we really have to go home? Waiting for his response was awful. I suppose there were hundreds more questions I could have wondered about, but he interrupted my analysis.

My dad broke into uncontrolled laughter. This was not the kind of laugh I'd hear when we watched the *Red Skelton Show* or even the *Three Stooges*. I can't truly say it was diabolical laughter, but it wasn't far from it. The only thing I can say for sure is that it had to stop. But it went on for blocks, though it felt like miles to me.

"There's nothing funny about this," I bellowed. He looked at me, still laughing. He regained control, his eyes pierced mine, and he quipped in some kind of sing-song way, "My son . . . doesn't have enough foresight . . . to be a box boy!"

A punctuating silence hung over the car as his message sunk in. Then at the same time, almost like we were members of a choir, we broke into all-out laughter. Our delight didn't end until we got home. By the time we arrived, I wasn't even worried about my mom's reaction.

I'd thought I was facing the end of the world because I'd been fired, but my dad knew it was just a minor bump in the road. Furthermore, we both knew I wasn't as stupid as the guy who just got fired. Well, at least I knew it. My dad trivialized the transaction and helped me see that even though my former boss said I lacked foresight, I wasn't stupid, I did have skills, and an important lesson had just unfolded in my life.

It wasn't just my father's language—his tone of voice also said he didn't think I was stupid. He thought I was a teenager, and teenagers make mistakes. He didn't judge me for them. I understood what his reaction meant. Not only did I have enough foresight to be a grocery store box boy, my future held bigger plans.

His one pointed remark turned a terrible situation into a positive one, and I realized that my life wasn't over because I was fired from a grocery store. I was a vulnerable teenager, as all are, and I needed someone with a larger perspective to reassure me of the obvious. Years later, I could really see things from my father's perspective.

My father was just one of many people who have influenced my life and have taught me a thing or two about important lessons that I hold dear to this day. These lessons I now pass on to my players. Throughout this book you will be reading in detail about these life lessons. It should be noted that all of these life lessons originate from personal experience and from family, friends, and loved ones who have taught me over the years the life lessons they've learned. Before you read the future chapters on life lessons, I offer as introduction moments in my life where I first realized the significance these teachings would have on me personally. Hopefully, this will grant you more of an understanding of each lesson as well as my own life journey and philosophy.

Life Should Be Fun, and If Your Life Isn't Fun You Must Change It

My parents, Joseph Howard and Cora Jean Resler, were married in Portland where they grew up. My dad's father had a menial job with the Burlington railroad. His mom cleaned houses. They spent all their hard-earned money on the necessities of life. My mom's family ran a successful car dealership in Portland. They came from money, but they were wiped out by the Depression.

The two families were worlds apart. My grandmother on my mom's side viewed herself as a moneyed, cultured sort of royalty. She appeared to be unaware that all of the wealth was gone. My grandparents on my dad's side were the salt-of-the-earth types who would grind their way out of the dirt to live their life. They had no pretense. They just existed.

My parents' wedding rehearsal brought these two very different families together, under the same roof. It isn't easy to merge oil and water, but that was to be my parents' future. The rehearsal was almost as packed as the upcoming weekend ceremony would be. It seemed impossible to combine these poles-apart factions, but my father was always up for a challenge. My dad was the kind of guy who looked for the fun in everything. He took one look at the uncomfortable attendees and thought it would be a tragedy not to seize an opportunity to create a little mischief.

As the minister addressed the families, dad excused himself to the bathroom, where he removed his suit coat and hung it neatly on a stall door. Using the garbage can as a stool, he crawled out of the window and jumped down onto the church lawn, which was being watered by several sprinklers. Grabbing two sprinklers, he placed one on the porch at the church's front entrance; another imprisoned the attendees at the back entrance.

Dad vaulted himself up and back through the bathroom window, smoothed the wrinkles from his black slacks, grabbed his coat and calmly went back to finish the rehearsal. The rehearsal proceeded in the usual boring manner. It was finally time to leave. Given the awkward tensions, compounded by the lengthy rehearsal, everybody wanted out. I suspect my dad was most looking forward to the departure.

I was never told how the families discovered their sprinkler dilemma. I know that once they found the problem, the only way the guests could resolve it was to become a team. They had to work together to decide how they'd fix this soggy situation. Should they all just quickly run out and through the sprinklers? They knew they had to decide who would go out first and turn off the sprinklers.

Being immensely noble, my dad volunteered to run through the sprinklers. He was capable of covering his tracks.

The older attendees, including my mother's parents, were offended and irate when they figured out the prank. Every time my mom told me this story though, she couldn't help but laugh. I suspect she knew the real culprit from the start. To her, that was her Howie, and that's why she loved him.

All of my childhood I watched my dad pursuing devilish delight in everyday situations. Laughter was at the center stage of our family. Nothing was out of bounds—nothing, as long as no one was hurt in the joking. I learned from my dad that every problem is only a solution waiting to be discovered. Furthermore, there must be a way to have fun solving the problem.

Like my father, I chase down fun with unrelenting passion. For example, when I started as Roosevelt's head coach, a very good friend of mine, Sam Lee, became the head coach at Juanita High School, another school in our league. Sam is the kind of friend I could tell anything to and he wouldn't judge. He has as sick a sense of humor as I have and, like me, the pursuit of fun is paramount. If I needed help, he would be there before the ball hit the floor.

Juanita's team had ranked last place in the league for years. Sam was hired to break the pattern, and his team was in the very early stages of the rebuilding process.

Sam, who'd lost almost as much hair as I had by that time, got a toupee between his first and second year as head coach. He chose to go first class, and if people hadn't known him before, they wouldn't know he had a toupee. I was surprised he did so because he ambles through life like everything is perfect and sweet. Just as my dad recognized the opportunity to have fun with the sprinklers at his wedding rehearsal, I knew the cosmos had offered up a fantastic opportunity in Sam's new toupee.

When a matchup was scheduled between Juanita and Roosevelt, it was time to get to work. Sherry, my wife and partner in crime, created 12 horrific toupees fashioned from black felt. Each hairpiece was adorned on either side by black sideburns, and a rubber band under the chin held the toupee in place. They were completely ridiculous. I met with the girls in the locker room and explained that they would wear these eyesores throughout warm-ups prior to the game.

The girls were worried that our prank would hurt Sam's feelings. Certainly these are laudable emotions, but I explained that Sam is the kind of guy who constantly searches for humor. It would never matter whether he was the prankster or the prankstee. He can take a joke. "Whatever you are doing in life, try to make it as much fun as you can," I explained. "You never want to hurt someone and, trust me, Sam will like this as much as we do."

My players started warm-ups nervous and reticent. When they saw the Juanita parents almost crying with laughter, they relaxed a bit. And pretty soon they were really into it. Sideburns flapping like wings, they ran boldly up and down the court, jumping and tearing at the basket. When warm-ups were over, they strode over to Sam and each girl handed him her toupee. Sam laughed his tail off.

I believe that when a game ends, both teams should enjoy basketball. There is no doubt that the Juanita girls were very afraid before the game. Roosevelt was a much better team, and no one is comfortable when Goliath walks into the gym. But our silly prank relaxed everyone in the gym, including our opponents. Honestly, that was not the plan, but that surprising silver lining made the game way more competitive and much more enjoyable for everyone.

Do you think any player can recall their stats from that game? I can't even recall the final score. But I know that every girl will remember how much fun we had preparing that gag because in life, you remember the intense moments. If I focused only on Xs and Os, my players wouldn't have nearly as much fun. Only when coaches combine fun and fundamentals—in that order—can they create winning attitudes.

I'd like to take credit for the lessons I teach, and for the times when someone I've taught has achieved success, or made it through a difficult time by applying one of my life lessons. But the lessons aren't mine alone. Like most kids, I have passed on what my parents taught me.

Share Your Talents

When I was in elementary school, I was a handful. During the first couple of weeks, my teachers liked me and appreciated my exuberance. However, it didn't take long before they learned that my mouth rarely closed and lacked a filter. "Bill" and "quiet" are words rarely in the same sentence, unless the word "not" is included in the middle.

And my no-filter mouth went off even in the most sacred of places. Each Sunday, my parents sent my sister, Judi, and me to the Church of the Brethren—not because they were churchgoers themselves, rather because they wanted at least one morning without constant noise. Alas, I suspect it wasn't my sister they were trying to

Still, I was the neighborhood underdog. When Gary wasn't ound, I'd go to the basket and practice. I learned all his moves. nfortunately, he knew mine. Therefore, I worked on developing new .oves. I developed a great running left-handed hook shot. I needed .e hook shot for several reasons: the hoop was on a hill and the down- .ill side was the left side of the basket; I was left-handed so I tended to .perate on the low end of the court; and Gary was four inches taller .han I was. I had to practice a ton because, quite simply, Gary was .nore athletic. He was Wilt Chamberlain and I was Bill Resler. Other .han those issues, I was in good shape. That's the good news. The bad .ews? I never beat him, but I was a competitor. Final score after more .han 1,000 games: Bill 0, Gary 1,000,000, or so it felt.

Gary was an assistant principal at Lake Washington High in the .ate 1990s, when their team was Roosevelt's chief rival. When I rolled into his gym, he was stunned to see me and even more shocked to see that I was a *basketball* coach.

I told my assistant coaches about Gary's undefeated high school record against me. No one was surprised, but we all laughed about it. At halftime, Gary was talking to some of his cronies when I approached him. One of his friends asked, "Is it true that you never beat Gary at one-on-one?" I nodded yes, and everyone guffawed. I looked at Gary and said, "We have a few minutes before the second half. Are you ready?" Luckily for me, Gary declined. Eight years later, I am still wondering if I can claim that as my lone victory.

As a Franklin sophomore, I was convinced I'd make the basketball team. I thought of myself as the best athlete around. Not only had I played basketball every day, I was also the playground's best quarterback in football, or so I thought. I was quick as a tortoise in high school, but my thought was that as long as I worked hard on defense, they couldn't cut me from basketball. I was wrong. They did.

The problem was, I was so painfully slow it didn't matter how hard I worked. Like most teenagers, I believed I was always right, and went to assistant coach Frank Ahern to explain his profound mistake in cutting me loose.

exorcise from the home. My dad knew there was a church two blocks from our home. What he didn't know is that Brethrens are pacifists. I believe that after a certain age, youngsters have a tendency to listen more closely to teachers and mentors than they listen to their parents. This is why teaching or coaching is such an enormous responsibility.

When I first entered the Church of the Brethren, I came from a family that had voted Republican in nearly every election, with a father who constantly spoke of how disappointed he was for not being able to serve his country in World War II. When you're six or seven years old, you listen to almost anybody but your parents. At the Church, the message I heard constantly as a five-year-old was that it's never right to kill anything, let alone humans. Instead of fighting, one could find a resolution through peaceful discussion. Thankfully, my parents left me in the care of pacifists instead of the Nazi youth. The pacifism stuck.

I remember being a six-year-old, sitting with about a half dozen kids in the Church of the Brethren's basement listening to the Sunday school teacher preach about Jonah and the whale, and other fables. Jonah and the whale is a Bible story about a guy who attempted to escape God by ship and was thrown to sea during a terrible storm. The Sunday school teacher earnestly believed God sent a whale to swallow Jonah, and only after Jonah prayed to God was he saved.

"Do you really think that guy jumped in a whale's mouth and lived?" I asked, interrupting her conclusion. "Wouldn't it be better if you told me a story I can believe?"

I aggravated even the pacifists. But some of their teachings stuck.

My personal philosophy about pacifism developed over time, but its foundation came at the Church of the Brethren. Personally, I could never take someone's life. I have no problem with people who are willing to (soldiers, police officers, politicians)—that is their position. I do not judge. I don't feel I have the power to decide other beings' right to life. My basketball players marvel when they watch me give them a major essay on aggression and then place a spider that wandered into our gym on a piece of paper and escort it outside to the bushes.

The Church of the Brethren was a very forgiving group. Constant references to forgiveness gave me the idea that we all make mistakes and, when we do, we should be forgiven and should be encouraged to fix those mistakes.

I teach my players to have all-out aggression on every possession, which seems contradictory to what I learned at church. But the messages to the players are metaphorical. When I tell them to sink their teeth in the opponents' necks and draw blood, I know they won't actually do it. The phrase "all-out aggression on every possession" has more meaning than just "be aggressive." Instead, every possession, every moment should be intense.

Many people have a negative view of aggression. Unbridled aggression is a negative act, but protecting our turf and those we care about is a worthwhile goal. As a pacifist, I am often questioned about why I preach such fierce and aggressive defense. As the Brethrens taught me, pacifism is a viable approach to life, even if it's coupled with ferocious aggression, and must come with caring humanitarianism. Forgiveness, pacifism, humanitarianism, and aggression are reasonable traits that can be garnered in one's youth.

My father, though, wasn't always in agreement with the Church of the Brethren's beliefs, though he was a pacifist in his own ways. Despite my attendance at the Church of the Brethren school, my dad wasn't a fervent believer in God. In fact, he called himself a druid. He often went hunting with his buddies, but never brought a gun. Instead he shot scenery with his camera. However, despite his views on the Church, when he had heard that neighbors were building the Church of the Brethren two blocks from our house, he eagerly contributed countless hours and sore muscles helping them, despite his own skeptical views of their religion. He was always more than willing to saw and hammer, but he wasn't willing to listen to what they were preaching. I guess druids are like that.

Why then did he help build their church? It certainly wasn't out of religious guilt. He helped them because it was the right thing to do as a member of the community. He was good with hammers and

saws and possessed endurance reserved for long-dis[tance] And he was willing to share those skills.

If you're intelligent, you're lucky. If you're g[ood] athletic, you're lucky. If you have parents who love [and] fully watch over you, you're very, very lucky. Time [and time] dad told me these things, and he also emphasized [sharing] lucky people. "When you're older, Bill, you have a [to share] your luck." I've heard that phrase so many times I'd li[ke] In fact, I've heard it so many times I don't think I eve[r] it. But as my players can tell, even worse, when I got o[lder] repeating it.

At the end of each Roosevelt basketball season, I [write] to the team's seniors. I tell each one how skilled she is f[rom] to the varsity—an accomplishment hundreds of girls d[esire] only a handful get to experience. I tell seniors how pr[oud] them and their journeys. In each letter, I tell them how lu[cky] for the abilities they have, and how they need to share t[hem] with others when they're older.

I can't be arrogant for inheriting my mom's photogra[phic] ory or my dad's charisma. I didn't do anything to earn th[em] know that I have many skills, but those skills pale in com[parison] what my parents taught me—that I must share my talen[ts] certainly hope I do through my coaching.

You Can't Have a Championship Team Without Sacrifice

When I was young, there was a basketball hoop three blocks home, and almost every day the 20 or so kids in our neigh[bor]would congregate there. My one-on-one rival was Gary Ma[rcus,] buddy who was one year older and lived a block away fro[m me.] was 5-foot-10 and 145 pounds as a sophomore. Gary was a [6-foot-] 2, 200-plus pound lineman on Franklin High's football tea[m. He] could have sent me to the emergency room with one leg an[d both] arms tied behind his back.

"You don't understand," I pleaded. "I'll *kill* myself on defense. You have no idea how badly I want to play. Use me as a practice player. I don't care if I get into games. I just want to play basketball." He let me stay.

Coach Ahern pulled me aside in the gym after a week. I was so obviously out of place; he explained that he had a duty to the team to fill the hardwood with the best players possible. Apparently, this didn't include me. I was cut again on what was truly one of the most rotten Fridays of my life.

I came back Monday and presented my case. The coach let me hang around for a few more practices. Eventually, I was told to stay home. Although I was tremendously slow of foot, I was pretty quick of mind so I told the team what I thought of their plays from the sidelines. I managed to get back on the team using my mouth, not with athleticism.

Being banned from the sidelines was devastating, and I didn't understand. And I especially didn't understand why I was also cut from the football team, when I believed I was clearly the school's best quarterback. Seven years later, when Tom Greenlee—the player they took instead of me—was named an All-American defensive end at the University of Washington, I reluctantly had to confess I might have overestimated my athleticism.

When *The Heart of the Game* was in its infancy, a local newspaper ran an article about the movie. In it, I mentioned being cut from Franklin High's basketball team. During my second year as Roosevelt's head coach, I attended the state playoffs, even though we failed to qualify. Between games, I bumped into Coach Ahern, who stopped and shook my hand. "Bill," he said, "I'm so sorry I cut you."

He'd read the newspaper article in which I'd talked about how painful it was to be cut. It was fine, I told my old high school coach. I went on to tell him that because he cut me from the team in a careful way, he'd made the situation easier for me. Looking back, this experience taught me how critical certain moments like this one are to teenagers, and how important it is to keep their self-confidence intact.

Cutting players is the worst part of being a coach. Each year, I dread the third day of tryouts when I call each girl over and have to tell some that they can't play Roughrider basketball. Customarily, they cry. And when I go home, I cry too. Trust me: on that night, I am no fun to be around. Many coaches print lists of the girls who make the various teams. If your name isn't on a list, you're cut. My positive experience with Frank Ahern taught me to carefully explain to girls which team level they've made, and why. Additionally, if I have to cut a girl, I explain in detail why there is not a spot for her at Roosevelt.

I know that every year, there are girls at Roosevelt who want to be part of a playoff team and never get to be. I know how devastating that can be, because during my senior year at Franklin, the basketball team won all but three of their league games and made the playoffs. However, everybody who is successful has taken a few hits. Such moments of sacrifice are inevitable. Basketball is like life: you can't have a championship team without sacrifice.

Work as a Team, but Own Your Own Life

I enrolled at Washington State University in the fall of 1963, partly because it was a good school; mostly because it was far from home and my family could afford the tuition.

In my second week there, I pledged the Tau Kappa Epsilon fraternity. The group of about 70 of us living in the house became an extended family. We spent so much time together that, for better or worse, we became true brothers.

The seniors ran the house, the freshmen did all the grunt work, and any personality flaw you had was dramatically exposed, often to the point where you either fixed it or caved to the pressure and left the house. Stories were told of your flaws or you were nicknamed. Once we introduced a guy as Sterile Darryl. No further explanation was needed.

As a member of the Tekes (our nickname), I was part of a team. And the team had expectations. But we also had fun.

Our house was extremely competitive, and those who stayed are still like brothers. Those who didn't share the team-first mentality moved on. There were guys who were wrapped in blankets and taken out in the boonies. Others were thrown into showers. Sometimes the seniors would stage a "wake-up." Wake-ups were fairly random, and usually occurred when the frat house got too dirty or maybe the seniors went out to a bar. A wake-up usually started when one of our brothers fired up a Harley-Davidson in the wee hours of the morning, followed by a lot of yelling and screaming. After humiliating the underclassmen for a while, the seniors would go back to bed and the pledges would clean the house from top to bottom.

A whole lot of camaraderie was created by these crazy antics. We learned through trial and error that being a team works. Not for a second though do I agree with these tactics. The goal was reasonable, but the approach was not, as it was hurtful.

One very valuable insight came out of this: you must take care of yourself to be able to care for others. Some pledges would go so hard during wake-ups that exhaustion overtook them. If they'd paced themselves, they would have been able team members until the wake-up ended. We learned that the entire team needs all members to step up. So if I saw a teammate struggling, I felt it my duty to help that individual, even if it caused extreme exertion on my part. You have to be part of the team, and sometimes that's not easy.

My older fraternity brothers weren't trying to scar us by exposing our flaws. They were trying to motivate us to correct them and make us better people. They knew that if we didn't become strong enough to own our own territory in the fraternity, we wouldn't be strong enough to own our own territory in other aspects of our lives. There wasn't a plan for these goals. If only our senior fraternity brothers had used less malicious tactics to employ this . . .

Teaching my young players to own their own life and also to bend to the will of the team is very difficult. There's a fine and often indistinguishable line between taking care of yourself and bending to the team's resolve. In life and basketball, job number one is to own your own turf. You must nurture it, push it, work on self-improvement, and be relentless in your pursuit of excellence.

At the same time, there is still job number two: make your team-mates better. They are both extremely important aspects of success. It isn't always easy to pursue your individual dream while functioning to create the dream for the team as a whole. There is enormous value in learning how to rely on others. It is equally significant to learn to let others rely upon you. This aspect of what it means to be part of a team should never be overlooked.

Never Give Up

I joined the outlandish Tau Kappa Epsilon fraternity because I fancied myself as a major young intellectual. At least that's what I told my parents. The Tekes had the worst grade point average among fraternities, sororities, and dormitories for five out of my eight semesters at WSU. Luckily, there were no stats about apartment dwellers. But we were better in some aspects. For instance, we were only on social probation for a mere three semesters.

I had one of the highest GPAs in my pledge class with a whopping 2.91. Alas, I fell off after that. I graduated with a 1.97 junior-senior GPA. It wasn't because my major was so demanding, unless you believe General Studies is demanding. The only reason my grades were lacking is that I didn't study and didn't go to class. At least I showed up for most of the exams.

You might wrongly conclude that I was just another frat boy slacker out drinking beer and telling stories. No, I was on a mission. I was learning to play bridge.

I finished school in 1967 when the Vietnam War was claiming thousands of my peers, and being an ultra left-wing pacifist, I had a moral duty to avoid the military. Graduate school was an obvious choice. It's amazing how educated a society can become when they start drafting college students for war.

In 1967, the easiest graduate school to get into was law school. So I studied my tail off for the LSAT, the law school entrance exam.

Despite my low transcript marks, I scored 707 out of 800, the highest among Washington State University students that year, and one of the state's best.

Chicago Law School had an agreement with WSU that the student with the highest LSAT would receive a full scholarship to their fine institution, which was one of the nation's top five law schools and is still among the best. Once they saw my transcript, I glumly discovered that the agreement was not binding.

I applied to Yale Law because I had one of the nation's best LSAT scores and maybe they were looking for someone different than your typical high-GPA student. They sent me a rejection letter within a week.

Even the University of Washington rejected me immediately, which was a demoralizing blow because at the time I thought they'd accept a one-armed lemur as long as it came with a high LSAT score. When the rejection letter arrived at the TKE house, I immediately called the University of Washington Law School to set up an appointment. I flew across the state a week later to meet the assistant dean of their law school and explained that there's more to a person's life than what you see on paper. I wasn't perfect, I explained, but nobody is.

He rejected me. The University of Washington was willing to stand by their original decision. I was, apparently, sub-lemur.

I arranged another meeting about two weeks later, and knew that if he didn't accept me, I might spend the years I should have been playing cards in law school stuck in prison for refusing to be drafted. The assistant dean was two sentences into explaining why he couldn't and wouldn't accept me when I stood up and slammed my fist on his desk. "You don't get it!" I said, pointing at him. "I went to a party school when I was 18 years old. I didn't know it was a party school. However, once I was there, I excelled at their culture. I'll be as good at any culture."

I pointed to the shelves of books behind him on that daunting Friday afternoon. "Give me the books to any course you teach. I'll study over the weekend and take a test on Monday. If I do well, you'll admit me. If I do poorly, you'll never have to see me again. But if you don't do that, you're going to have to call the police, because I'm not leaving until you admit me, or give me a chance to be admitted."

"We aren't questioning your ability," he said. "We're questioning your motivation." I jumped up and threw my arms out. "Do I look unmotivated to you?"

My arguments were persuasive. In the years succeeding, not only would I graduate from the University of Washington Law School, but from there would study taxation at New York University School of Law Graduate Tax Program—then the nation's top program and still one of the best. Thirty years after convincing the Washington law school dean I was capable, I became the director of the graduate tax program in the University of Washington's School of Business.

You should not be judged by your mistakes. You should be judged by how you fix your mistakes. How many times have we heard, "To err is human; to forgive is divine." I could not disagree more with that ridiculous thought. Yes, to err is human. Forgiveness is mandatory!

As an educator, I am involved in the process of student improvement. As a coach, I must set the bar high to substantially increase improvement. During the process, things will go wrong and sometimes teenagers believe that the hurdles blocking their way are insurmountable. As their coach, I break problems down into basic elements and shower the players with encouragement, always reminding them to never give up.

Inch by Inch, Life's a Cinch; Yard by Yard, Life Is Hard

Some of life's obstacles are impossible to avoid. In 1968, during my law studies at University of Washington, I was drafted by the army. That year was an ugly one for draft legislation. School was no longer a get-out-of-jail-free card for draft exemption, unless you studied healing sciences. I am pretty capable of crafting clever arguments, but I couldn't quite spin law school as a healing science. After several conscientious objector appeals, in November of that year I was an available quarry, and a perfect target for the draft. I was 23, and when it came to the draft, the older you were, the higher your priority until age 26. During that stage of the draft, anyone 26 or older felt like they were shooting free throws and living tax-free.

In mid-December, a surprise arrived in my mailbox: my acceptance into the Army Reserve at Seattle's Fort Lawton. Right on! That guaranteed that I would not have to violate my pacifist views or go to jail as a conscientious objector. But nature imposes a quirky sense of humor. Next to the Reserve acceptance letter was a letter from the army. It was my draft notice.

It was now time to put my law training into action to figure out which letter had priority. Put in bridge terms: which letter trumped the other one? I uncovered that it was the date of mailing—not the date of delivery—that determined which had priority. My draft notice had been sent a day earlier.

For sixth months I did everything I could to appeal my commitment into the army. In a last-ditch effort, I found a telephone number for Washington State senator Warren G. Magnuson and called him on a Saturday morning. "You're not an American if you won't support your country," he told me.

I struggled to explain, but Senator Magnuson had had just about enough of me. To this day, I get a little queasy about that mean-spirited dial tone. And, by the way, I don't much care for Magnuson Park in northeast Seattle either.

I was supposed to report to the army in February 1969, so I went to the dean of the University of Washington law school, Laverne Rieke, and explained that I wanted to finish the winter quarter before reporting for boot camp. Besides putting off basic training, I also wanted to take shorthand and typing at Seattle Community College to improve my clerk skills.

On the first day of my community college shorthand class, there were 23 women and me. Normally I'd be in heaven as the only man in a class with so many women, but that changed when the women found out the main purpose why I was there. The instructor asked each student to tell the class why they were taking shorthand. I was the last to speak and willingly blurted out, "I've been drafted and I am improving my clerical skills so that I might be a clerk instead of in the infantry." They couldn't mask their disgust. Their faces and body language seemed to indicate that there were 23 women and one little boy in Shorthand 101.

When I received my draft orders, I interviewed people who'd already served to find out what I'd be up against and what I should do. The dozen or so people I talked to told me that all soldiers are tested during the first week of basic training to determine where they would be assigned. I knew it would be the most important moment in the army and was sure there were only two outcomes for me: clerk or prison. I was told that if any leader asked a group of soldiers if anyone has been in ROTC, I should eagerly raise my hand. These seemed backwards to me. Shouldn't the proper strategy be to be as low a profile as possible? I wanted to be the invisible stealth soldier whose only weapon was a typewriter.

On April 14, 1969, most of us were deeply depressed as we boarded the bus for Fort Lewis, about an hour south of Seattle. We wondered how on earth we got stuck there. We rode silently as the bus left Seattle behind, and headed south for God-knows-what. When we departed the dreadful bus, we crossed the threshold from civilian life into army existence. There were piles of duffle bags lying around among the chaos. Sergeants yelling, troops running: one could believe we were on the set of a movie titled *300 Stooges*. Except that it wasn't funny.

"You better pull your head out of your ass, troop!" a sergeant kindly suggested to me. This was something I heard a lot during the Teke house wake-ups, and unfortunately the sergeant's comment caused me to laugh. Judging by what happened next, it was not the response he was hoping for. He was now yelling more obscenities than I know directly into my right ear. I was amazed to learn that my 165-pound weakling frame could tote three duffle bags up three flights of stairs. I doubt I'll ever be able to do that again.

There were 55 guys in my platoon. About 30 of them were happy to be there, because it meant waking up without a hangover. The other 25 were college graduates who had been extremely happy to wake up *with* a hangover.

Our first platoon meeting commenced at 5:30 a.m. Drill sergeant Fox asked, "Has anyone here been in ROTC?" Ouch! So soon. Well, I had pretty much abandoned the crawling-silently-in-the-grass gambit, so what the hey . . . I raised my hand.

"Reezler, you're a squad leader," he said flatly. Everybody don your rally hats, squad leader Resler was making a comeback. Drill sergeant Fox didn't really like me, but I was the only one who'd raised his hand.

Now, sometimes the truth is not so easy to discern because of gray areas and back eddies where truth and fiction get confused. Technically, one could argue that I'd never been in the ROTC. In my freshman year at WSU, I signed up for ROTC because a senior in the house told me to because he was in ROTC. As a rookie, I didn't want to butt heads with any of my senior brothers.

When I went to the ROTC field house to get my uniform, there was a long line of freshmen guys funneling into a building. I got in line and attempted to chat with other fellas on queue, but wasn't making much headway. It began to dawn on me that these military types were not quite the same as me.

After a day of being taught with the yell-till-you're-hoarse-and-then-yell-some-more methodology, I started home. As I walked the 15 or so blocks back to my fraternity, my army dress hat kept falling out of my bundle. Each time it hit the ground, I was closer to quitting ROTC. By the time I reached the TKE house, I'd returned to being a civilian and never endured another day of ROTC training.

Technically, a case could be made that I hadn't actually taken ROTC, but at boot camp drill sergeant Fox's question to my fledgling platoon was, "Has anyone here been in ROTC?" I'd raised my hand, but failed to mention, um, that I hadn't been in ROTC for very long.

One morning at boot camp, they gathered about 2,000 of us for a lecture on military law. Based on his previous behavior in basic training, I knew the lieutenant teaching the course didn't know diddly-squat about military law, and most likely anything else for that matter. This lecture came about seven days into basic training and already this lieutenant was hated by 99.44 percent of the troops. He acted like a know-it-all banty rooster that probably should have been laying eggs.

Oops! That same hard-to-be-around kid with a no filter-mouth had now been through two years of law school, which included a course on military law. There was trouble brewing in the armed-forces air.

The lieutenant's lecture was straight from some instructor's book, and he told us that once you get caught in the military justice system, "your civil rights are gone." His statement was almost accurate, but he should have said, "Once you're involved in military law, you've probably lost your civil rights." I raised my hand.

"What about a collateral attack via the writ of habeas corpus, which will put you outside military law?" I'd just about used up all of my barely known legal jargon in one sentence. A writ of habeas corpus is a judicial mandate ordering that an inmate be brought to the court so it can be determined whether the inmate is imprisoned lawfully.

"I'm unfamiliar with that," he said. "Well," I explained, "if you do the research you'll correct your error." The troops went wild, especially given that this particular lieutenant was loathed by us grunts.

I was soon thereafter assigned to be a military clerk for 19 months at Fort Lewis. My year and a half of law school got me to headquarters, where they made me a legal clerk—a job that held enormous power. Check out my base duties: process evidence for a case, recommend to a colonel what charges should be brought, type up the charges, assign the defense counsel, assign the prosecutor, assign the judge, and process the judge's holding. So much for checks and balances.

At the start of my army experience, with my pacifistic views on life, I had dreaded my entry into service. There was no way I was ever going to fight and kill anybody. But I stuck with it, took each challenge day by day, and made headway in my work as a military legal clerk.

If I had tried to deal with the army as a whole, the well-oiled system would have worn me down. So I took each challenge head-on and did my best. In basketball, it takes a huge array of skills to become a solid player. My job as coach is to break these skills down into small, manageable packages. I point out constantly when my players work on these drills why inch-by-inch matters. By managing small conquests, they are building foundations for larger skills that will eventually become easier to acquire.

Failure Is Achieving All of Your Goals: It Means You Didn't Aim High Enough

After my time in the army, I returned to law school with a good conduct medal for serving my country. Even better, I carried with me one of my greatest memories from the awards ceremony: I didn't go.

I didn't go to law school classes either because by then I didn't want to be a lawyer. But what else was I supposed to do after being in the army for two years? I drifted through school—again.

My personal property securities class was taught by Warren Shattuck, a University of Washington legend who I was told drafted major contracts for Boeing, and was one of the nation's best contractual law professors. He was also known for being hard as hell—so much so that whoever received the highest score on his final exam was given $75 and a book on personal property security law.

I took the class during a summer quarter and on the first day, Shattuck announced it would be the first quarter in his career that he wouldn't take or require attendance. So I never went to his class again.

About five weeks into the quarter there was a note on the law school's main bulletin board directing me to see professor Shattuck. "You have to drop the class," he told me. I asked why. "You haven't been to class yet," he replied. "Well, how did you know I wasn't there?" I baited him. "There was never anyone sitting in your assigned seat," my professor said.

Well, this didn't make sense so I came back with, "How could I sign the seating chart if I wasn't there? I was there the first day when you said we don't have to come to class anymore." My childish reasoning didn't work. "You'd better come to every class from here on out," he demanded. "I can't," I said. "When you told me I didn't have to come to class, I got a job, and my hours there are the same as your class. You've put me in a bind."

"You have to come to class from here on out," he said, with unwavering anger. But I would not bend and retorted, "In my contracts course I was taught the concept of promissory estoppel; that if you have estopped somebody from doing something, you can't go back on your word. You misled me by telling me I don't have to come to class, so you're promissory estopped from demanding that I change my life." Not surprisingly, he dismissed me from his office in a not-too-friendly manner.

I didn't read the study materials Shattuck had written himself (the packet was about two and a half inches thick). Nor did I buy Shattuck's book. I figured there had to be something on the course in the college library.

I found a book that was about 20 pages long. It was about four-by-six inches—a perfect nutshell of personal property security. The night before the test, I tried to commit this book to memory. Of course, I was only aiming at short-term memory because I had no plans to practice law. All I had to do was absorb a sufficient amount of information to get through the four-hour final exam.

The test's first question completely baffled me, and I was desperate for at least partial credit to pass. "I'm completely confused by your set of facts here," I wrote. "I can't tell what the relationship is between the parties." I went through every detail of the four possible scenarios—lease, contract, executory contract, and a landlord/tenant agreement—and fessed up that I didn't know the end result.

The instructor graded the tests without knowing which student's paper he was grading, and the grades were posted about three weeks later. Word had gotten around that nobody had failed, so I was no longer afraid when I went to check the scores. I was shocked to find I had the highest score out of about 40 students. The question was a trick. The facts were confusing on purpose in an attempt to make students explain all four scenarios. No one was lucky like me—no one else nailed it.

To my knowledge, that was the only quarter that Shattuck didn't give out the $75 and book to the highest scorer. When I said "hi" to Shattuck in the hall, he acted like I was invisible. I thought it was a sweet victory and the ultimate compliment: the rules had been changed to defeat me, but his dastardly plan had failed.

My dad worked for the Internal Revenue Service, which in my mind almost guaranteed I would never choose anything relating to taxes as a profession. However, I felt I needed to take at least one tax course in law school because I wanted to be conversant in my dad's chosen career.

Almost all law school courses are based in logic. If I punch a guy in the face, I'll end up paying that guy some money. If I breach a contract, I'll owe something for breaching the contract. Almost all law courses have a certain amount of common sense to them. Tax law is the complete opposite.

My tax law course so confused me that I had no idea in the world what was going on. And my ego doesn't allow me to be conquered by anything. I knew that in most law classes, I could spend a few hours memorizing materials and regurgitate the information to get a decent grade. But in my tax course, I felt completely lost. When I was forced to study that crazy, convoluted stuff, I realized, "Hey, tax law is pretty cool."

When I graduated from law school in 1972, the nation's best graduate tax law program was at New York University, so I applied. About two weeks after I sent in my formal application, I got a formal reply. Essentially, they stated, "We have a lot of excellent candidates, and you're not one of them."

Frustrated, I went to professor Ron Hjorth, who had taught my tax course at Washington. He motivated me by pushing me so hard, my ego was challenged. "That's the best program in America and you have never demonstrated anything that would allow you to go there," he told me.

"But how'd I do at tax?" I asked.

"You did well in that class, but were terrible in your others," he said, referencing near-failing grades in contracts and commercial law courses.

I told him I wasn't going to class because I didn't care about being a lawyer. I only finished law school on default. When I discovered tax law, though, the subject interested me as a potential career. I also wasn't programmed to be second place, and I was not going to settle for the second-best graduate law school in taxation.

Ron Hjorth believed what I told him, and agreed to write a letter of recommendation. "If Resler likes your program," Hjorth wrote, "he'll be one of your best students. If he doesn't, he'll be the worst. It's not a question of whether or not he has the ability; it's whether or not your program is good enough to motivate him." His letter and my own letter of explanation helped me get accepted to NYU a month later.

I aimed at the best thing possible using a bipolar approach. At times, I demonstrated some real academic horsepower. Other times, I sent a message to the world that I didn't seem to give a damn about anything. I'd pulled down the awe-inspiring 1.97 junior–senior GPA from WSU, and backed that up with below-average grades in my first two years of law school. On the other hand, during my third year in law school after returning from the army, I'd conquered the monster LSAT and won an academic award for being the law class's most improved student. By being perceived as hopeless in the eyes of my professors and classmates, I had much more room to improve.

To obtain considerable achievements, you need to aim high. To be a 4.0 student you need to aim for a 5.0. I try to make each day perfect and attempt to make each day better than yesterday. I never succeed on the first try and rarely succeed on the second attempt, but my daily efforts are vastly improved by the intensity of chasing those goals. I prefer perfection, but don't expect it.

I often tell my basketball players that the team that makes the most mistakes usually wins the game. They find that hard to believe, but by taking risks and pushing themselves to amazing heights, mistakes are more probable. However, when such risk-taking pays off, the depth of achievement will be considerable.

Work Hard, Play Hard; Don't Get the Two Confused and Move Quickly from One to the Other

I could skip an entire semester of classes as an undergrad, show up for the final, and still pass thanks to luck and the memory inherited from my mother. At NYU, it was a different world.

Every weekday, I'd be sitting in a library cubicle at 8 a.m., when the law library opened. Excluding the hours I was in class, I would stay in my cubicle until 8 p.m. I packed sack lunches and sack dinners and ate them in my cubicle while I studied. I'd return for another eight hours on the weekend. There were no exceptions.

When 8 p.m. rolled around, I'd emerge from my hole to explore the city. I'd only live in NYC for nine months, and I was not going to limit my sightseeing to cubicles and classrooms. On weekends, I'd walk for hours exploring the town, not thinking about classes for a second.

One of my most favorite memories of my time in Manhattan was the day four of my buddies and I took our friend Sarah Meeker to McSorley's Old Ale House for some beers.

Sarah was a ballsy, say-anything-at-any-time kind of woman. She was outrageously good-looking, and even better, she was outrageously cool. A speakeasy during Prohibition days, McSorley's is one of the oldest bars in Manhattan, with nostalgia-enducing swing-doors and sawdust-covered floors. Just weeks before we took Sarah to McSorley's, a law was passed that required the bar to allow women patrons. My buddies and I knew there was no better woman to take than Sarah.

The law didn't require gender-specific bathrooms, so McSorley's owners kept only one as a way of sticking their tongue out at society. You can imagine what that bathroom was like when Sarah had to go.

When Sarah emerged from the bathroom, she held up two middle fingers for all to see. She didn't care what anybody thought of her, and the bar erupted with laughter.

Here was a woman who was strong enough to hold her own, yet she knew that having fun was the way she would break down sexism, if only temporarily. That night, she was the primary reason everyone was having fun.

My balance of work and play allowed me to make the most of my nine months in New York. During my time at NYU, seven A+ grades were given. I earned three of them.

Everybody has heard the phrase "Work hard, play hard." But I believe in "Work hard, play hard. Don't get the two confused and move quickly from one to the other." When you play, have more fun than ten clowns, but when you're working, be extremely efficient. You'll enjoy your tasks more because you're focused.

I graduated from NYU in 1972 and was offered a job on the faculty during my last semester. Most of my colleagues taught one tax course for two or three consecutive years. In my two years as an NYU professor, I taught four.

I didn't take on the extra workload for bragging rights. I did it because when you teach a subject, you learn it far better than you would as a student, and I wanted my students to be able to ask questions outside of an individual course.

At the end of my second year, my dad was dying so I returned to Seattle to be with him. Although I loved New York City, which had the most fascinating, go-crazy-all-the-time environment, I couldn't imagine returning. New York City didn't have the Cascades. It didn't have Puget Sound. It didn't have recreational opportunities like the Northwest did.

So I took a job at a law firm in Seattle with John Cooper, one of my closest friends from law school. Cooper was an ace, but my boss was the worst card dealt. We saw eye to eye on almost nothing and like most people, I'm not productive when I'm not happy. I know that life should be fun, and when it isn't fun, you should change it. So I did.

I left the firm after less than two years to become dean of the Seattle branch of Golden Gate University School of Taxation. In 1978, a year after starting at Golden Gate, I filled in at the University of Washington as an adjunct professor. I was asked to stay full time that year, but turned down the offer because of my commitment to Golden Gate and because I had my own law practice. The Washington faculty tried to lure me away each year, but I didn't realize my true calling until 1983 when I was hired.

By 1983, I'd practiced tax law for seven years and couldn't stand it. I loved the subject, but couldn't stand the greed that consumed my clients. It bothered me so much that by the time I'd completed a case, I couldn't stand to be around those clients.

Finally, I met with accounting department chair Bill Felix at the University of Washington Business School and told him I was going to take a major pay cut because I thought teaching was my calling. "We'd been hoping you'd make that decision," Bill told me.

Years earlier, Gerry Wallace, my mentor at NYU, hoped for the same thing. I was 27 when I asked Gerry, director of the NYU Graduate Tax Law School, for a recommendation letter during my final semester. "Have you ever thought about staying here?" he asked.

I told him I'd interviewed with several New York law firms, but wasn't really interested because most the people I interviewed with seemed to have drastically different perspectives. "I meant stay here, as a professor," he said. I told him that wouldn't be good for me or for the students, most of whom were older than I.

"Do you think I'm a good teacher?" he asked.

"I think you're a great teacher," I replied.

"Then trust me," he said. "You'll be a good teacher."

Because I am not particularly concerned about making mistakes, I have been able to take risks to improve my teaching and coaching methods. When I set my goals, I break down the elements that are essential to achieving the goals and pursue the mastering of these elements with as much vigor as I can muster. Having chased these lessons throughout my life, I believe I've improved my ability to teach them.

The successes I've had and the mistakes I've made allow me to anticipate where many of the mistakes will surface with my players, daughters, and students. Anticipating their foibles allows me to prepare for teaching them how to correct their mistakes. In my first eight seasons as head coach, Roosevelt collected a 163–49 record, earned four KingCo titles and five state tournament berths. Roosevelt's record is better than any other KingCo team in that eight-year time period, and I have become the most successful girls coach in Roughrider history. All three of my daughters are extremely successful young women with powerful self-esteem. I was lucky enough to become an award-winning professor at the University of Washington. I know there was no way I could have accomplished those feats on my own, and I honestly don't judge my successes by plaques, awards, and trophies. The success was not born out of basic talent; instead, it is an embodiment of the life lessons I've learned over the years and which I in turn present in this book.

CHAPTER TWO

The Inner Circle

Senior Allison Reiman leads an Inner Circle meeting in the summer of 2006. (Photograph by Casey McNerthney)

CHAPTER TWO

The Inner Circle

Senior Allison Reiman leads an Inner Circle meeting in the summer of 2006. (Photograph by Casey McNerthney)

Empowering Your Players

I was seven years old when I first tasted the importance of empowering those you teach. It was recess time for my first-grade class on a typical fall Seattle day—pouring rain. I suppose it was implied that we shouldn't go outside and play, but apparently I wasn't issued anything that resembled common sense. When I strolled back into the classroom looking like I had jumped in Lake Washington, my teacher spanked me with a paddle in front of the class. After two somewhat predictable whacks, I picked up on her timing. Before she could whack me a third time, I rolled off her leg, causing her to slam the paddle into her lap. I wasn't surprised when she sent me to the principal's office amid the symphony of kids' laughter. King Prankster was making another trip to the head guy's office, and by that point I was on a first-name basis with the principal for reasons no parent would be proud of. So, I wasn't afraid to reason with my old buddy. "You know, I shouldn't get hit with a paddle because I went out and played in the rain," I told him. "I've already been punished—I have to be wet all day."

"Yeah, I know," my principal said. "Just make sure when you leave here that everybody knows I scolded you really severely." He explained why the teacher was upset, and explained that I had the power to go outside, but in some instances it wasn't the best decision. It was my decision, he said. The principal told me in words a first-grader could understand that I was responsible for my own actions. He showed that he trusted me and his lesson was one I still think of often: if you empower the person you're with, they get more out of the lesson you are trying to teach them. However, I didn't fully realize how much this experience taught me until years later when I became a parent, teacher, and coach.

My oldest daughter, Jessica, was born in 1979. Alexa was born two years later, and Vanessa was born in 1983. From the time they were little, my wife and I allowed our girls full votes over anything that was not crucial. When they were six, they didn't get to vote on who drives the car. But where we would go to dinner, what we would do for fun—that was all fair game. My wife and I were usually outvoted 3–2. We went to Chuck E. Cheese's far more times in a month than any parent wants to in a lifetime. But we endured those frighteningly loud robotic characters and endless rounds of "Happy Birthday" because we were teaching our girls to make choices and to be responsible for their actions.

There were neighbors who said we should have vetoed at least a few evenings at Chuck E. Cheese's. But that's ridiculous. A veto would have destroyed their power. It's the same as asking whether your kids should have a lock on their bedroom door. The answer is "of course." Kids need a sanctuary, a retreat that they can claim as their own. My daughters had locks on their doors from the time they were toddlers, but there was a hole to unlock it in case of an emergency. Allowing them to have their own territory was another form of empowerment. Because they had a proprietary stake in the outcome of many family decisions, our girls learned that to achieve great results, they needed to make smart choices.

When Vanessa was in second grade, I volunteered to coach basketball for ten boys and ten girls at her elementary school on Thursday afternoons. The kids were so young that there was no league to enter them into, so at the end of our season of practices the kids played the parents. In order to level the playing field, I required the parents to only use bounce passes. When they shot, they had to be on their knees to give the kids a chance to block it. This also gave the kids a great chance for fast breaks, since it took a little time for the older folks to get back up on their feet and get moving after taking a shot. The parents built up a double-digit lead, and *somehow* blew it. In the fourth quarter, an unspoken conspiracy amongst parents transformed their team into an absolute mess. I'll be darned if the kids didn't win on a last-second layin, and their celebration was to die for.

My daughter Vanessa and her older sisters, Alexa and Jessica, all played basketball, but Vanessa was the one who fell in love with the game. When Vanessa was in fifth grade, she asked that I start a select team, which I did with Bryan Willison, who later became my assistant coach at Roosevelt. Vanessa was a guard, and all of her friends were on that team. We played more than 90 games per year in weekend tournaments across the Northwest. In 1992, a parent who had watched me coach Vanessa's team asked me to coach a select team of seventh-grade girls for three weeks. The team had only four games scheduled, all in the Nordstrom Hoop Festival at what is now Key Arena.

The practices I designed were incredibly intense. At first, the seventh graders complained that my crazy practices drove them nuts. They went home after practice all red-faced and were too tired to hang out with friends. Nearly every drill ended with a winning team and a losing team, and I made the losers run or do pushups. For one drill, I'd toss the ball on the floor, a mad scramble would ensue, and whoever recovered it came out the winner. For another drill, I'd get three girls to hold on to the same ball and when I shouted, "Go!" the player who pulled the ball away from the other two girls was the victor. And once they were ready, I challenged their hoop-shot skills with contests in which they shot from their knees, from midcourt, from behind the backboard, and, while facing the backboard, from behind their back. The balls careened off wire-protected gym lights, smashed against walls and off the bodies of teammates. Balls flew everywhere, including out the gym doors and into the school hallways. But it was amazing how much fun the teenagers had while mutually failing.

We didn't scrimmage much; however, every drill was part of our overall offense or defensive scheme, which would pay off when we eventually did go up against an opposing team. We played a lot of three-on-three and I kept track of each team's stats. I mixed practice teams up constantly, so the girls played against and with a variety of teammates. At the end of the round robin three-on-three games, every girl had played against every other girl on the team. Records posted on the gym wall showed each girl's individual win-loss record. Since no girl wanted her name posted toward the bottom of the standings, the three-on-three battles became fiercely competitive. Over the course of these three weeks the girls developed pride, aggression, a sense that mistakes don't matter as long as you are trying hard, and knowledge of how to be a teammate.

All those tough practices paid off big-time—we crushed our first opponent by nearly 30 points. Our second game was against a team from Mt. Vernon, a rural town in northern Washington. If a home in Mt. Vernon lacked a basketball hoop, it meant there was no one under age 50 in the household. So there was no surprise when they battered us in the first half. When we were down by about 20 points, I told my team that we were going to lose that game but it didn't matter. "All those girls are going to go back to Mt. Vernon and they're going to say, 'City girls are wimps,'" I whined at them. And then I got tough. "You haven't knocked one person down. You haven't owned your area of the hardwood. They're going to go back home and say, 'You know those city girls just don't have it.' That's kind of embarrassing for you, I think. If I were you, I'd go out there and do whatever it takes so that even if we lose, at least they'll think that there are good athletes in Seattle." We hit a shot at the buzzer to win. I had tweaked their pride, and in the quest to show the other team they were athletic, they unleashed raw teenage spirit. It was my first lesson on how much spirit matters in basketball.

The Roosevelt junior varsity coach left after the 1994 season. Several girls from the Nordstrom Hoop Festival team that I coached played at Roosevelt, and they recommended me to varsity coach Aileen McManus, recalling to her the effective mix of intensity and fun they had during my practices. They told Aileen how much they enjoyed my coaching and that I'd raise the level of fun while infusing the Roosevelt program with a spirited aggression. (On a side note, my daughters were attending Roosevelt at the time, but they'd traded their Nikes in for grease paint. All three participated in the distinguished Roughrider drama program, and I couldn't have been prouder of them for making that independent decision.)

Aileen called and asked me to interview for the position. I did, but was concerned from the start about balancing my family, my director position at the University of Washington, and the commitment to the team. The JV coach was required to attend both the junior varsity and varsity practice daily, *and* attend games for each team at least twice a week. It didn't matter that the pay worked out to about $1.50 an hour—I was willing to forego the big dollars for community service. But I didn't want to give a half-hearted effort, so I passed on the offer.

I explained this to Aileen, saying that I would be glad to help out in another way: being water boy, carrying clipboards, or doing any other odd jobs that nobody else wanted. She countered by offering me the position as coach of the freshman team, called the JVC. The JVC practices last for an hour and a half immediately after the school's 2:30 dismissal, and the games were at about the same time. I would only have to mildly adjust my schedule.

Many of the JVC players were athletes—they just didn't have much experience at this difficult game. So I attempted to simplify the complexities of basketball for girls who hadn't spent hours on the court before high school. During our half-court practices next to the junior varsity, I worked to improve the girls' basic skills with passing, shooting, and defensive drills. I completely bypassed dribbling drills because passing is the key to the game, and if I'd let them dribble without sufficient skills, the more likely they were to turn the ball over by dribbling into a crowd, or dribbling out of bounds, or any of the other myriad things that can go wrong with indiscriminate dribbling.

Basketball and life are difficult, confusing, and complex, especially for teenagers. I believe life is easier when you take it one step at a time, especially when facing brand new challenges. It's my belief that when you're learning something new, it's best to master the essentials first. This way, you'll have solid skills and feel more confident, which can help you learn advanced skills more quickly and increase the odds for success.

I believe that when a game is over both teams should still like basketball. Employing that premise, the Roosevelt JVC didn't usually run a full-court press after the first quarter because we built too big of a lead. When we had controlling leads, we played a packed-in 2-3 zone defense so the other teams could get their shots off. But no matter how much we tried to avoid blowouts, we trounced a few teams. We racked up 43 points against Nathan Hale High's team, which didn't manage to make a single basket; Ingraham High scored a mere 8 points to our 56. Our only close game was a 7-point win against Franklin. The minimal-dribble offense worked because passing moved the ball faster than dribbling. Passing makes you see your teammates whereas dribbling tends to isolate a player.

As an aside, whether it is the championship game or merely a preseason game, I believe a high school coach should never run up the score. The coaches and parents from both teams should be there for all the girls and the referees. A 20- to 30-point win is plenty to assure a victory. It is very difficult to keep players from running up the score, though, because the girls will always want to play hard. To avoid blowouts, I've learned to do away with fast breaks and I usually impose a rule that we must pass seven times before we can shoot.

After my two successful seasons coaching the JVC, the Roosevelt JV coach departed our program for a better teaching position. I wasn't the advisor to the accounting honorary at the University of Washington anymore, so I had a bit more free time on my hands. I asked Aileen if I could be the JV coach. She explained that I would have to interview, but I had her support.

The interview consisted of about ten questions. I was asked how I'd handle things if the JVC coach couldn't make a practice, with 20 girls in the gym and only one coach. The Roosevelt athletic director wanted to know how I organized my practices. I produced an Excel spreadsheet detailing my organizational methods. He also wanted to know my views on winning and losing and other standard questions. During the interview, he and Aileen did not comment upon my answers because the Seattle Public Schools interview guidelines prevent that. Each interview must be identical in terms of questions. Later, Aileen told me that the athletic director chose me as the new JV coach based mainly on my sense of humor and energetic approach to the interview.

In my fourth year as an assistant to the varsity and my second year as JV coach, *The Seattle Times'* preseason preview reported that since we'd earned second in our league the previous season, the Roughriders had a chance of making it to the state tournament. Our team played as predicted, achieving an 18–3 start and a spot in the conference championship. The problem was that to win, we had to beat the Bothell High Cougars—a team ranked fifth in the state on a 17-game winning streak. Much worse, Aileen's father died of an unexpected heart attack days before the game, and she traveled to Eastern Washington to be with her family. The role of varsity coach was thrust upon me, and it was up to me to lead the team to victory at the championship game.

I had no doubt we could win, or that my coaching methods would work, but I did doubt the girls' faith in me. JV coaches rarely get the respect given to head coaches, and instructions from assistants are often dismissed like those of grade school substitute teachers. In preparation, I studied game film on Bothell for eight hours since they'd beaten us 58–48 earlier in the season. Bothell's star was Becki Ashbaugh, a 5-foot-6 senior guard who averaged 17.7 points per game. The game film exposed Bothell's strategy: teammates consistently shot the ball to Ashbaugh on all inbound plays. If we could keep that from happening, Bothell's game plan would collapse. I took three girls aside—Jade White, Amanda Ostrom, and Aimee Espiritu.

"You are the three assassins," I told them, "and you're going to rotate—two minutes in, four minutes out—guarding Becki Ashbaugh. And when you come out of the game after two minutes, you'd better be breathing really hard, because if you're not, you won't play any more. I expect two minutes of complete fury, and then you get four minutes of rest. None of you are allowed to shoot, because you're going to be too tired to shoot, except layins. If Becki Ashbaugh goes to get a hot dog, you're going to give her the mustard. If they take her out of the game, you're going to sit on the Bothell bench. If she goes to the bathroom, you're going to sit in the stall next to her. The three of you have the biggest responsibility in this game, and when you shut her down, we win. I'm sorry you're not going to get the same number of minutes that you usually get, but it's too important.

"If you listen to me, we won't just beat them, we'll slaughter them. But you're going to have to believe in me, and you're going to have to listen." The assassins, as I nicknamed them, accepted their mission.

The game was close in the first half, with the lead changing ten times. Then, just as we hoped, the assassins wore down Ashbaugh. She was held below her scoring average and the heavily favored Cougars never led in the second half. Roosevelt's 60–43 win brought home the school's first KingCo 4A championship and the top seed to the district tournament. Skill doesn't matter nearly as much as spirit does.

When the season was over, Aileen came to me and said she was going to resign as head coach. It was too much of a time commitment and there was too much pressure from parents, she said. I thought about it for a few weeks and told her that I was going to apply for the head coach position. Aileen told me that she was glad, and would support me any way she could. Because of our win over Bothell, several parents were also in favor of me being the head coach. Nearly a dozen other candidates had applied when I submitted my application because Roosevelt, located in an upper-middle-class section of Seattle, is arguably the best public school in the city. It wasn't clear to me that I was going to get the job, but to strengthen my application, I had several letters of recommendation from Roosevelt parents and one from outsider Sam Lee, whom I'd met through coaching select teams.

To be the head coach, you must go before a committee. The nine-person committee comprised several Roosevelt players, parents, and the athletic director. I went into the interview with the mindset that I was on my way to playing in the state championship. I readied for the interview like I was preparing to win the biggest game of my career.

The opening question was, "What's your coaching philosophy?" I asked if they meant coaching on a game-by-game basis, coaching philosophy over the course of a season, or coaching philosophy in terms of life lessons as they interrelate to basketball. This put the committee on their heels because they weren't anticipating that I'd analyze the question that way. The committee conferred, and told me they wanted my basic coaching philosophy. So I reached into my briefcase and whipped out printed copies of my response to that very question. As I handed them out to each interviewer I explained, "You can read this over while I give you my verbal description." I had anticipated six of the interview questions, so for each I provided the panel with printed copies of my responses.

One question I didn't anticipate was, "How will you prepare the girls for difficult losses?" I grinned at the panel and told them that I didn't expect to go undefeated in my career. Since I knew there were losses coming, I told them I'd prepare for losses before they occurred. When preparing teams for a potential loss, the most important thing is to explain that winning and losing isn't as important as being pre-pared to win. If you instill in players the idea that they didn't lose the game if they played their best, it lessens the pain of a difficult loss. I never tried to completely eliminate the pain of losing a game, because the experience of a heart-wrenching loss teaches us so much about life.

All of that preparation time must have been worth it, because out of many qualified candidates they gave me the job. While I was elated that I had been selected, a substantial fear and trepidation flowed through me. I was, once again, out of my comfort zone.

The most important goal for me as a coach—and in any teaching role—is to *empower* my charges. It's important to get students to believe in the learning process and to help them realize that when they own the process, it usually leads to success. I believe that all teachers should ground their work on this basic principle.

Early in my first year as head coach, I wanted to figure out if there was a method to further empower my players. I awoke one night with an intriguing question: if I gave my players free reign to control their team, making decisions that would dictate the results of their season, would they be able to learn the lessons and skills needed to make the team and themselves successful, and work through the problems that arise? If I gave the girls more power, their decisions and responsibilities for the sake of the team could create a stronger unit, and thus might make them more aware and responsible for what's at stake. I also realized that creating such a joint venture in team management with several bright teenage minds could yield much stronger decisions than anything my old brain alone could dictate. The next day at a meeting with the varsity team, I presented them with my concept, which I called the Inner Circle.

The Inner Circle consists of the 12 varsity players, who meet privately to share their thoughts and, through this interaction, make decisions. How Inner Circle meetings operate is not determined by me, because all my assistant coaches and I are not allowed to attend Inner Circle functions. The Inner Circle is about the players only, and as such, only the players can attend Inner Circle meetings. Therefore, the very foundation of the Inner Circle is ownership. By removing much of my power over the girls, they then can possess greater control over their team, causing them to believe in both their team as a whole and themselves as individuals. I strongly believe it's important that kids learn the value of shaping their own lives at an early age.

There are minimal rules about the Inner Circle. Meetings can begin at the coaches' behest, or the girls themselves can call for one. Inner Circle meetings most often occur when a varsity player tells me to depart in no uncertain terms, usually after I've made a decision they may not agree with. The girls typically retreat to the locker room, though the meetings can occur anywhere. Based on what I have heard from past players, some teams gather in an actual circle, while others are more laid-back and not so formal.

The most important rule of the Inner Circle: after meeting, a representative of the Inner Circle must inform me what the players have decided. While I sometimes ask why they made a decision, they are not obligated to tell me. Except on the rare occasion when their decisions are impossible to make, I am not allowed to veto an Inner Circle decision. To this day, I have never made a single veto.

Though empowering my players is the primary reason behind the Inner Circle concept, there is another motive for holding these meetings, which is to keep outside influences away from the court. As mentioned previously, the assistant coaches and I are not allowed to partake in these meetings, as our own personal motivations could corrupt their decision-making skills. But it's not just us who are barred.

Parents and friends are likewise not allowed in the Inner Circle. They are welcome and encouraged to attend practices so long as they don't distract the team's focus and intensity. Although we have this open-door policy, in actuality only a few parents attend. Thus, most parents have too little information on which to base a decision or a conclusion about the team. Most of what they know of team chemistry is hearsay from their daughters and what the parents observe during games. Furthermore, a small percentage of parents are far too involved in their daughters' athletic careers, so their bias could be a serious detriment to the decision-making process. The Inner Circle was designed in part to limit such parental influence on the team.

As you can imagine, this often doesn't sit well with some parents. Coaches are often criticized by parents. It's unrealistic to expect 12 sets of parents to agree with how one coach teaches basketball strategies. The Inner Circle adds another layer for parents to contend with. A few parents are constantly trying to erode the power of the Inner Circle, believing that their daughters don't have the ability to govern their young lives. To me, this is the most important reason to have the Inner Circle—to allow the girls to experiment with responsibility and leadership.

The team's outer circle consists of coaches and parents; these people are close to the athletes but are not actually on the team. A circle further outside includes such disruptions as people attempting to sell drugs to the players, trying to keep them from studying, and generally obfuscating the right decisions. The Inner Circle in its very essence eliminates all such distractions and maintains focus on teamwork.

Like the locks my daughters had on the doors of their childhood rooms, the Inner Circle shelters athletes from outside influences—those too removed from team chemistry to be useful for decision making. I've observed a close relationship between the teams' effective use of the Inner Circle and their successes on the court. I find it interesting that in my first eight years of coaching, the one year a team of mine did not use the Inner Circle also happened to be the only year we had a losing record.

At the beginning of each season since that very first one, I explain the purpose of the Inner Circle to the players: "This is for you as athletes to take charge of your team. The coaches will try to make top-notch judgments to make you the best team you can be, but in the end, it is your team and you make the decisions." It is then understood that the coaches will give players input during the season and help with technical development. But the cohesiveness of the team will ultimately be a result of their choices.

Through the years, I've witnessed a variety of ways in which the Inner Circle empowered young players. It has dealt with social problems, team disciplinary problems, and team procedural issues. I'm told that some Inner Circle meetings were ferocious arguments that began as screaming matches, but ended in reconciliation. Most teams have eagerly embraced the authority that flows from the Inner Circle and they are sometimes surprised by the extent of its power. I've seen the benefits of the Inner Circle so many times I can't count them all, but I've described below a few shining examples of how well it worked, not only for the players, but also for coaches and parents.

I've heard many tales of high school teams fiercely debating over which player should be designated team captain. I'm certain every time this scenario occurs there's at least one player left heartbroken, if not more. I'm against selecting a team captain because it can lead to hurt feelings and resentment amongst teammates, and hurt the team's performance.

Obviously, hurt feelings are a part of high school sports, but I don't agree with creating a situation that sets one player above all the others and triggers negative feelings in other players. To me, that seems as brilliant as throwing your son on the pavement to help him learn to deal with pain. If you think that's a good idea, then you and I aren't going to agree on much. When a player's feelings get hurt, I do believe there's a silver lining in that they'll learn from the experience. For example, when 50 girls try out for the team, a number of girls won't make the cut. They get upset and so do I, but this type of a decision is unavoidable. On the contrary, I believe that basketball teams don't *need* to have captains, and so I choose to avoid that situation altogether.

During my first season as head coach, the team had five amazingly dynamic seniors. Lindsey Wilson was pure athleticism and radiated an unrelenting desire to win. Rachel Nord was a magical joker who never let a practice slip by without making at least one player smile. The incredibly intense Jade White wowed us with her dynamic street smarts. Alaina Forbes could outwork the world, and if the moon were inhabited she'd outwork teams there, too. Remarkable healer Amanda Ostrom brought opposing factions together. Amanda's uncanny skill could bring the curtain down on the typical drama that permeates the fabric of any group of teenage girls. I was supposed to pick which one was better than the other? Not a chance. In my view, they all should have been named team captain. I also believed that a true leader doesn't need to own the official title of team captain for other players to follow her example. Why increase Kleenex's stock price over such an artificial title?

About four weeks into the season, the seniors came to me and told me that they were bickering over which players should act as spokeswoman for a given game when the referee called for the team captains. Lindsey, who led by example early in the off-season, insisted that we keep the same spokeswoman for an entire season, so it was obvious who our leaders were. I suggested that the seniors vote amongst themselves and figure out who the captain would be. Jade vetoed that immediately. She was adamant that it should be the choice of the entire team, not just the seniors. Anyone living within three miles of Roosevelt knew Lindsey was dying to be team captain. I also knew that if the other seniors didn't pick her as captain, there may be a huge rift in the team.

We faced the much-hated Redmond Mustangs in a few days and I knew we could lock them out only if each Roosevelt girl clicked like the tumblers in a safe. All of us believed that we owed Redmond a smackdown, as Redmond players had been claiming that the reason we were undefeated was we hadn't played any good teams yet. Unfortunately, we were caught in a hurricane of team drama. If we didn't play as a team, we'd be congratulating the Mustangs for snapping Roosevelt's perfect record. Two nights before the Redmond game, I received four phone calls at home from seniors who were not named Lindsey. Each one posited the concern that if Lindsey didn't act as captain for the all-important Redmond game, the team might explode in a multi-level meltdown. "You need to do what you believe is right," I offered. "If it's right that Lindsey is not a captain, then that's what you should do. If it costs you a few losses, it doesn't matter. What matters is what you believe." It still wasn't clear to me who the girls really wanted to be team captain, but I strongly felt that the decision didn't have to be based on wins and losses.

The next day after practice, I gave the seniors my counsel, then waited alone for about an hour as the Inner Circle made its first major decision in the Roosevelt locker room. As I waited in the gym,

I wasn't scared or nervous. I really didn't have very strong emotions because I didn't care what the outcome was. It was their team, and I would support any decision they made. For most teams, two players are chosen as the captains for the entire season. Who the Roughriders chose did not concern me because any of the five could have been strong leaders. When Amanda, the Inner Circle representative, came to me, I learned that the team decided that Lindsey would always be a captain. For the other captain position, the four remaining seniors would rotate into the role for all the remaining games. I consider that to be the wisest decision that they could've made. Furthermore, I think the girls understood that on some level, the leader of that team was going to be the leader, regardless of who was designated captain on any given night. They realized the title of captain didn't matter—team spirit did.

From time to time, my players were faced with an issue that required a second Inner Circle pow-wow in order to rethink a decision, and perhaps amend or change it. Halfway through my first season as varsity coach, we were beating teams by 30 or so points. My response to this was to start bringing JV players up to varsity games to give them some varsity game-time experience. It allowed them the chance to play in the big show and a chance to be scared, which all players go through when they hit their first varsity game. I was beginning to plan for the future.

The girls held an Inner Circle meeting without my knowledge. After they had met secretly, a bunch of players approached me insisting that I meet with the team. But they didn't tell me what the meeting was about. All I knew at this point was they demanded my attention. After practice, we met in the locker room, me at the front and the team in a U-shape around me.

The team wanted my attention and they wanted it yesterday. Sometimes the Inner Circle messenger briefly informs me of their choices. I had no such luck this time. The varsity girls felt that because I'd brought some JV players to play in games, they weren't getting sufficient playing time. The seniors were especially bothered because this was their final season at Roosevelt and they wanted more time on the hardwood. I told the team that I was extremely proud of them because I always want my players to desire more minutes. That's part of a basketball player's passion for the game. For about 30 minutes, I kicked through my decision-making process, trying to explain that the future matters just as much as the present. But if we're playing a dependably inferior team, I said, the most skilled varsity players aren't learning much from the experience. I mentioned that there were two varsity players who I'm certain weren't playing as much as they believed they deserved to. I then pointed out that neither of them had uttered a word about it. They could have chimed in with their teammates' whining (and no varsity coach would have been surprised if they did), but their team-first attitude was a major reason for our success, I explained.

After I gave my reasoning, the team asked me to leave and gathered for another Inner Circle meeting. The seniors later came to me and announced that the team understood and accepted everything that I had said. However, they wanted to make sure I understood that we should have fewer JV players on the court as we neared the playoffs, and that I should be reasonable about JV playing time. One thing I liked more than our undefeated record at midseason was the fact that they trusted me to be reasonable. Something I liked even more was that the seniors assured me I would hear from the Inner Circle again if they felt I wasn't being reasonable.

Another of my favorite Inner Circle stories began with Meghan Miller, a 2001 graduate, who was one of the most dynamic of all the athletic girls in the history of the Roosevelt girls basketball program. Meghan's reflexes were as quick as I will ever know and she was as smart as any person I've ever met, posing the question of which was quicker: her mind or her reflexes. Trust me, she would resolve the debate before I could come close to an answer. On defense, Meghan's amazing reflexes allowed her to not just block passes, she would intercept them even though she was only four feet from the passer. She made it look effortless, like she was merely playing catch with the opponent. Meghan wasn't afraid to dive like a superhero for a steal, regardless of the score. She had the kind of I-am-Wonder-Woman attitude that made even the opposing crowd roar when she flew through the air. Meghan had a 4.0 GPA, and played the piano and the trumpet in the award-winning Roosevelt jazz band. She was a three-year all-league soccer goalie in high school, and earned a scholarship to the University of Kansas where she was a second team All-American goalie.

In December of Meghan's junior year, she went to Florida during basketball season for a select soccer tournament. My personal view of it was: I don't ask the girls who play both basketball and soccer to go to basketball tournaments during the soccer season. And I don't believe they should be made to play soccer during basketball season if it interferes with the basketball team. I didn't fuss when Meghan told me she was going to miss practice. It was her choice. Of course, I ran the hell out of her when she came back, because that's what happens to anybody who misses practice for whatever reason.

I met with Meghan and her parents in the spring before her senior year and told them that by playing soccer during basketball season, Meghan was seriously compromising her commitment to the team. I told them that this was unacceptable. Meghan and her parents understood my concerns, agreed that she could not jeopardize the team's success by playing soccer, and assured me that she would not go to Florida during basketball season again.

Early in her senior season, Meghan pulled me aside after practice and informed me that she was going to the same soccer tournament again that year. She was meek and embarrassed, and stared at the floor. I was shocked and a little angry because Meghan had broken her promise to me and her teammates. In spite of her timid recalcitrance, I told her I might have to cut her because the trip violated team rules, and she had broken the promise she'd made the previous April. I knew from the start that Meghan's college sport was going to be soccer, and basketball was something she did for fun. She wanted to go to the tournament because she'd made a commitment to her select soccer team, but she'd also made a commitment to her Roosevelt hoops teammates, and most importantly, it was basketball season.

I decided to cut Meghan after four days of painful deliberation with the Roosevelt coaching staff. I could have told Meghan my decision right away, but I waited for a few days, a tactic that has served me well in my professional career. Many of my students at the University of Washington must choose between job offers from two firms. I always tell each student the same thing: choose a firm, picture yourself working there, and then if you're still in love with the job after imagining yourself on that firm's dime for a week, call the firm immediately to accept their offer. So I often employ this same tactic as a coach, and Meghan's case was perfect for this decision-making style. I had to wear this decision for a few days to assure myself that it was the correct fit.

I finally took Meghan aside and told her that I might have to cut her from the team. Her eyes shot a shell-shocked arrow right through my eyes, deep into my soul. I was sad to give her the news, and scared of how this might adversely affect her life. On the other hand, Meghan had abandoned her basketball team after promising not to, and I had to deliver the decision that the coaching staff thought was justified.

Meghan told Emily Watson, a close friend on the team, and Emily told the other teammates what I had done. Four girls approached me before the next practice and asked why I was cutting Meghan. I cited my conversation with Meghan and her parents before the season, explaining that she could not violate the commitment to her basketball team by attending the soccer tournament. The next day, Emily and several others told me the team was going to hold an Inner Circle meeting without Meghan. I shot baskets in the Roosevelt gym for two hours after practice awaiting their decision. Usually, I don't fret much about an Inner Circle meeting. That day was different, because it wasn't a ministerial decision such as creating team captains.

The Inner Circle representative told me that I could not cut Meghan, but that due to her actions, Meghan would be in my doghouse as long as I thought it was reasonable. She'd pay the price according to what I believed was correct, I was told. It was one of the proudest moments of my life. The girls had stood up for their friend and teammate, knowing that Meghan was an essential part of a winning team. They also trusted me to be reasonable in my dealings with Meghan while she was in my doghouse. Meghan, who waited for the outcome in a small room near the locker room, was honored by what her teammates had done for her. She was so honored that she refused to leave them for the soccer tournament, even though soccer was her career sport. How did her soccer coach reward one of her best players for being loyal to her basketball teammates during the basketball season? She cut her.

I didn't get the decision right. It was the Inner Circle that showed that 12 minds of the teenage persuasion are far more skilled than that of one old man. Imagine how good the soccer team could have been if they had an Inner Circle.

In my second year as head coach, three athletes riding in the same car showed up one minute late to a pre-game walk-through, which is held an hour before tip-off. During a walk-through, we literally walk through all of our inbound plays, side-out plays, and offensive sets. While missing a minute of a walk-through isn't crucial, coaches must teach punctuality. Whenever a player is late, the team runs a Sweet 16, a conditioning exercise in which players sprint from sideline to sideline 16 times in less than a minute while dribbling. Even the most dedicated players despise the drill. It's even worse for the player who let her teammates down: she has to stand at center court while her teammates run by her.

I didn't tell the team of their impending punishment before the game because the girls would have lost their focus. After we had won and I gave the post-game talk, I explained the importance of punctuality and told them the team would run three Sweet 16s at the next practice. The girls stared through me with steely eyes and demanded that I leave the locker room. The Inner Circle had spoken. I returned to the deserted court and wondered what decision would greet me when they called me back into the locker room.

When I returned 15 minutes later, they declared that they would not run the three Sweet 16s. Here was an interesting problem I'd never faced before. The Inner Circle had legislated away one of our constitutional rules: if you're late, it means the entire team runs, period. I was considering how to address their decision, but the girls weren't through filling me in on their reasoning yet. They added that if anybody showed up late from here on out, the entire team would run three Sweet 16s in addition to the three they were avoiding this time. Once again, 12 young brains outwitted one old one. They impressed upon themselves the importance of punctuality and team camaraderie, and did it through their own actions using the Inner Circle. That was a far better outcome than if they'd acquiesced and just run the original punishment Sweet 16s.

Girls later showed up 15 or 20 minutes early for everything. If practice started at 8:00 a.m. on a Saturday, they would be there at 7:45. Instead of being at games 60 minutes before game time, they appeared 75 minutes early because they didn't want to let their teammates down. I don't know this for sure, but they probably showed up at 2:15 a.m. instead of 2:30 to encase my house in toilet paper.

They never ran those Sweet 16s. The Inner Circle came through, as it almost always does.

I believe the most effective way to educate teenagers is by allowing them to learn through experience. I think it would be impossible to truly teach decision-making by lecturing teenagers about how exactly to make specific decisions. The Inner Circle allows them to make decisions as a group and learn from the lessons that come with the decision-making process. Some of the Inner Circle's decisions may be the most important in their lives at that time; consequently, they pour their hearts and souls into the choices they make.

I know that when my players become adults and community leaders, they will have to make group decisions. I suspect they will be strong leaders due to the training the Inner Circle gave them in high school. And as some of the upcoming chapters demonstrate, the benefits of the Inner Circle have made my players stronger people.

CHAPTER THREE

Lindsey Wilson

Lindsey Wilson (Photograph by Casey McNerthney)

ranklin prevented it. So in the summer between her
nd junior year, Lindsey Wilson enrolled at Roosevelt.
got the call from then head coach Aileen McManus,
gasted. Roosevelt hadn't qualified for a state tourna-
than 15 years, and even then the Roughriders lost both
layed. I knew Lindsey could be the catalyst that could
to state, and possibly advance our team past the first
e first time in Roosevelt's history. But I was also con-
what would happen to team chemistry. We already had
li Izidor, who was voted league player of the year the
on for her 18.5 regular-season scoring average. I didn't
sey's take-charge persona would match with Enjoli and
mmates.

al, high school teams have two kinds of players: dedi-
s, and students who are there for social reasons. It's not
or even the most dedicated players to take a couple days
nmer. But it wasn't in Lindsey's character to take a day
ticed every day for hours at a time wherever there was
t.

of her off-season work, Lindsey made double-digit scor-
ok easy during her junior year. In a much-anticipated
t Inglemoor, she scored 16 of her game-high 28 points
quarter. She turned heads again five days later when she
n-high 19 points in a 59–49 win against Woodinville. In
e against Franklin, her former team, she played only 22
he 32-minute game, but scored an impressive 18 points
victory (which extended our record to 9–0).

hemistry was like a hydrogen bond—the players were
gether but could explode at any moment. The veteran
ayers were happy to have Lindsey because we added a
punch and a girl who gave a damn about winning. On
nd, a popular senior had been demoted from her start-
because of Lindsey, so their feelings were mixed. Players
this behind Lindsey's back while she took classes at

Share Your Talents

I know I'm very lucky to coach at Roosevelt. And I know that the inherent skill that helps me be a successful coach comes from just that: luck. My parents taught me that if you're intelligent, you're lucky. If you're good-looking or athletic, you're lucky. If your parents love you and carefully watch over you, you're very, very lucky. And each lucky person has a duty to share their talents.

Teenagers often have a difficult time learning to let others rely on them, which is another way to share one's talents. Being part of a team is a terrific way to garner that skill. When teens learn to rely on each other as teammates, the results are often awe-inspiring. I believe the lessons players learn about teamwork on the basketball court won't disappear after the final buzzer. Lindsey Wilson was one of the most talented high school players I've ever seen. As an individual, she was as impressive. When she learned to share her talents, she became legendary.

As a Roosevelt assistant coach during the 1995–96 season, I had seen the newspaper clips about Lindsey Wilson, a phenom freshman from Franklin High. She joined a team that took second place at the state championship the previous season, but the coach put her in as a starter almost immediately because of her awesome moves. When the Franklin Quakers played a rematch against Blanchet High, the team that beat them for the state title, Lindsey came off the bench to score a team-high 13 points. She consistently scored in double-digits, which provoked the Franklin coach to start her in that season's Metro League championship.

Roosevelt was a team with exceptional talent, led by all-league quick forward Enjoli Izidor, who earned a basketball scholarship to Stanford University. Our chance for a post-season berth came in a must-win game against Franklin. It was my first chance to see Lindsey Wilson in the Roosevelt gym, and if I hadn't been on the Roughrider bench, I would have liked what I saw. Lindsey chewed up our defense, and spit out a team-high scoring performance. She drove like an upperclassman, hit pull-up jumpers, left our players in the dust with spin moves, and made circus-act layins look easy. Franklin left our house with a 48–44 win. Without Lindsey, I doubt they would have.

Lindsey also excelled her sophomore year, and it was a rare game when she didn't score in double digits. It seemed every time I picked up the high school sports page, there was a story about how she spearheaded another victory for the Quakers, ranked by *The Seattle Times* as the city's best high school team that year. Roosevelt played Franklin twice that season, and in each meeting Lindsey mauled us. She wanted to score every time she had the ball in her hands. If an opponent covered her close, she'd use her amazing court vision to get the ball to someone else. In my first eight seasons as coach, I saw only two players with Lindsey's ability: Darnellia Russell (see Chapter 10), a senior in 2004, and Darnellia's freshman teammate, Ariel Evans.

Lindsey's the kind of girl who would rather swallow glass shards than lose. The only thing she hates more than losing is knowing that she didn't work as hard as possible. She grew up in Seattle with two brothers, five and six years older than her. All three kids inherited athletic ability from their dad, Bruce, a standout high school line-backer who later played at the University of Washington. Lindsey's

brothers didn't treat her like a ⸱⸱⸱
them long before she could d⸱⸱⸱
brother's bedroom door. Whe⸱⸱⸱
game until Lindsey was 16, w⸱⸱⸱
of watching their sons check ⸱⸱⸱
walls lining the driveway.

Lindsey credits her tough⸱⸱⸱
tered by the big brothers who⸱⸱⸱
started playing on select sport⸱⸱⸱
star of her soccer team, Linds⸱⸱⸱
1993 USATF National Junior C⸱⸱⸱
But basketball was her best s⸱⸱⸱
knew she wanted to play profe⸱⸱⸱

Both Lindsey's brothers ⸱⸱⸱
chanting the Quaker cheers. Al⸱⸱⸱
friends attended Franklin, and⸱⸱⸱
dropped participation in all ⸱⸱⸱
establish herself as the city's b⸱⸱⸱
eight hours a day, and she hate⸱⸱⸱
week when she could have b⸱⸱⸱
5-foot-7, Lindsey knew she di⸱⸱⸱
she turned heads because she c⸱⸱⸱
same type of work ethic that ⸱⸱⸱
different level than other playe⸱⸱⸱

Though her double-digit sc⸱⸱⸱
selection, Lindsey wasn't happy⸱⸱⸱
her teammates wanted individ⸱⸱⸱
ment, Lindsey later told me. It ⸱⸱⸱
ducive to improving her game, ⸱⸱⸱
didn't sit well with her black tea⸱⸱⸱
ing an inner-city school, was the⸱⸱⸱
the first time in her life that she⸱⸱⸱

Lindsey also wanted to take ⸱⸱⸱
College to earn her high schoo⸱⸱⸱

time from ⸱⸱⸱
sophomore ⸱⸱⸱

When ⸱⸱⸱
I was flabbe⸱⸱⸱
ment in mo⸱⸱⸱
games they ⸱⸱⸱
help take u⸱⸱⸱
round for t⸱⸱⸱
cerned abo⸱⸱⸱
a star in En⸱⸱⸱
previous sea⸱⸱⸱
know if Lin⸱⸱⸱
the other te⸱⸱⸱

In gene⸱⸱⸱
cated athlet⸱⸱⸱
uncommon⸱⸱⸱
off in the s⸱⸱⸱
off. She pra⸱⸱⸱
an open co⸱⸱⸱

Becaus⸱⸱⸱
ing efforts ⸱⸱⸱
game again⸱⸱⸱
in the four⸱⸱⸱
scored a te⸱⸱⸱
her first ga⸱⸱⸱
minutes of ⸱⸱⸱
in the 70–4⸱⸱⸱

Team ⸱⸱⸱
attracted t⸱⸱⸱
Roosevelt ⸱⸱⸱
true scorin⸱⸱⸱
the other ⸱⸱⸱
ing positio⸱⸱⸱
talked abo⸱⸱⸱

North Seattle Community College. Since all of Lindsey's classes were off campus, she wasn't around to hear her teammates' hallway bickering. As such she couldn't head off what was being said about her, even if it was just typical teenage squabbling, the type that existed when I was in high school and I expect will still be part of the high school experience when Lindsey's great-granddaughters roam those halls. It's the hallways where the fabric of team spirit is shredded and rewound over and over during the course of any season.

At 9–0, we had been at the top of the league standings, but soon the team play that took us to the top dissipated. A 61–56, double-overtime loss to Lake Washington, then our most bitter rival, dropped the Roughriders to 11–2. Though we were still one of the state's best teams, the chemistry wasn't the same. Lindsey told me later that after that tough loss, her teammates pulled her aside and told her she wasn't passing the ball enough. They were tired of watching her try to win games by herself and the frustration had finally surfaced. The smoldering hallway prattle finally took down the team.

Though Lindsey was learning to share her talents with her new teammates, she would only do so for those willing to work as hard as she did. However, very few, if any, worked at that level. For teammates not at that level, she didn't care to share anything. She needed to learn to share with each teammate, even if she had a dissimilar work ethic. She was the one who took at least 1,000 shots per day in the off-season. She logged more hours in the weight room than the entire team combined during the summer. She wasn't afraid to drive into an opponent. She made nearly all her layins, and could shoot a three-pointer with a jump shot, while most high school players are only able to shoot a three-pointer with a set shot. She mastered every offensive move and refused to give them up because she knew she needed to take up the slack for teammates who didn't work as hard as she did.

Lindsey kept playing just as hard and as well as she had all season, but she still wasn't aware that the team was suffering because she was not sharing her talents with everyone. In a rematch with

Inglemoor High, she and Enjoli each scored a game-high 24 points to snap the Vikings' eight-game winning streak. She led scorers with 20 points in a 62–48 bashing of Redmond, and scored 21 in an upset against Bothell that earned Roosevelt the top seed in the bi-district tournament. As Lindsey still likes to remind me, she never lost a game in Roosevelt's gym no matter which team she played for.

In 2002, veteran *Seattle Times* reporter Craig Smith said he'd never heard of a girls team in any sport with a higher percentage of future college athletes than our team that year. Lindsey and three others were future Division I basketball players, and two others went on to play soccer at Division I schools. Ten players went on to be college athletes, which explains why we won the KingCo 4A championship in a year when every team in the league had a headline-grabbing superstar.

During the playoffs, the Roughriders' back-biting continued to poison the team's chemistry. Some parents were critical of Aileen as head coach, so much that one held a secret team meeting to give the team a pep talk. I delivered a speech before our loser-out game in the bi-district tournament at the University of Washington, telling the team that it was our home court, and our opponents from rural Snohomish would be timid in the city. We owned the gym and we would own them, I told the girls. But they were wound so tightly that my words fell useless on the locker room floor. I'd never seen them play so flat. Enjoli gave us a two-point lead with 3:54 remaining, but when time expired Snohomish beat us 50–46 and Enjoli sobbed uncontrollably at center court. At that point, I wasn't thinking about what the next season would be like. All I knew was that Lindsey had to share her talents with each of her teammates; otherwise there was no way we'd be successful.

The following spring, Aileen told me she was going to resign as head coach because the time commitment was too intense and she was tired of constant pressure from parents. I applied for the job, and when I was hired one of the first things I knew I had to address was how to make Lindsey more of a team player.

Enjoli had graduated, and Lindsey was now the Roughriders' undisputed star. Next in line was junior Devon Crosby-Helms, who scored 15 points and 12 rebounds in a 60–57 win against Lake Washington the previous season to put Roosevelt in the league championship game. Months before the 1998–99 season started, I took Lindsey, Devon, their parents, and their select team coaches out to dinner.

I called them together to tell them what I thought was the truth: I didn't feel Lindsey respected her teammates, and that had to change. She didn't like to pass, and when she did she passed to Devon, whom she played with on a select team. No team can afford a caste system, I said.

Lindsey had a stone-faced reaction to my speech, and the adults' looks told me it was a bit awkward that I launched into the speech without small talk. I explained that in terms of talent Lindsey and Devon were like NBA teammates Michael Jordan and Scottie Pippen, respectively, and that Lindsey was on the path to becoming the Michael Jordan of Washington state high school basketball. But unlike Jordan and Pippen, Lindsey and Devon weren't taking full advantage of the team. "And it will be really unfortunate if the state's best player sits on the bench in most games because she doesn't value her teammates."

One of her select team coaches said that Jordan and Pippen had a more talented supporting cast. "This is another example of you not knowing anything about Roosevelt," I told him. "Because if Jordan and Pippen left, the Bulls would be a losing team. If Devon and Lindsey leave, we'll still be a winning team. So don't tell me they don't have teammates to pass the ball to. We'll just be way better if Lindsey and Devon share the ball the way Jordan and Pippen do."

Lindsey said she did care about her teammates and my opinion wasn't accurate. I gave the example of a recent open gym when she didn't sit out for a second, even though there were more than a dozen players waiting for playing time. Any player that cared about her teammates would sub herself out, I said. Lindsey's dad completely understood the flaw there, and explained why he was upset with Lindsey for her actions. Without the support of the parents, I don't think my message would have been understood and accepted by the girls.

During her senior year, Lindsey started taking classes at Roosevelt in addition to her classes at North Seattle Community College. That gave her time with teammates in the hallways, which created a chance for stronger team chemistry.

I've never met a player, including Angela Nefcy, with a stronger work ethic than Lindsey Wilson. (See Chapter 5 for more on Angela and her game). Lindsey was a girl who, during the off-season, did leg-numbing conditioning drills most girls despise even during the regular season. Every so often, I'd ask the team during practice if they were working hard enough to be champions. It didn't matter if Lindsey was soaked in sweat, near the point of exhaustion. She'd always bellowed "no," preceded by a four-letter modifier.

During a practice in her senior year, a player on the Roosevelt boys team called her a bitch. Though she was smaller, Lindsey wasn't intimidated and didn't tattle to a coach. She responded by punching him in the face. The boy she hit later confronted her at school, and though only words were exchanged in the hallway, her select team coaches showed up at the Roosevelt boys practice that afternoon. These two built guys in their forties told the teenager that if he got near Lindsey again they'd slit his throat, which corroborates why I didn't care for those select coaches. A few years later, one was sentenced to 40 months in jail for statutory rape.

Lindsey was suspended from school for punching the boy and because of her select coaches' antics. The suspension meant she'd miss two exhibition games, and players weren't sure what would happen with the team's natural leader gone. It turned out to be one of the best things that happened to our team all season.

We crushed both teams without Lindsey. No girl took her place as the star—each just executed exactly what we practiced. Our backcourt press frustrated opponents. Players weren't hesitant to share the ball with teammates. We made almost all our free throws. The girls learned that they were an amazing team on their own, and with Lindsey they were even better. I hoped Lindsey would realize she wasn't a one-woman team and would see the need to share her talents with her less-talented teammates.

But later that season, Lindsey relapsed. During one of our games against Port Angeles High, players from Bainbridge High who were to compete against Port Angeles the following week were there to scout the game. About a half dozen of the players on Bainbridge's team had played select basketball with Lindsey. That game she played selfish basketball, showboating for her friends. Though all her tricks— behind-the-back passes, crossovers, no-look passes, beyond-the-arc shots—were working that day, after a quarter I'd seen enough. I benched her and tore into her with a rich vocabulary.

"I don't give a damn about your friends from Bainbridge," I said. "You're done for the game until you explain to me that you won't do that showboating stuff anymore. Because if you pull that stuff again, you have no idea what I'll do."

A few days later, we were to play Monroe, which had been considered one of the state's top ten teams. Walking out of the locker room, Lindsey approached me and slung her arm over my shoulder. "Bill, I thought about it all weekend, and you're right," she said. "I haven't been valuing my teammates. I've spent the entire offseason turning myself into the best player in the state of Washington, but I forgot that my primary duty is to make my teammates the best they can be."

Teenagers thank you when you bring treats to practice. They thank you when you don't make them run conditioning drills. Almost never does a teenager say to an adult, "Thank you for criticizing me. I really needed that information, and it will help me grow." I was quite touched by Lindsey's statement, because I realized it was her way of saying thank you.

We blew out Monroe so brutally that the Monroe parents applauded when we scored. When the dust settled, we had won 71–46. Lindsey had 13 points and a career-high 13 assists. Monroe coach Alan Dickson came up and shook my hand. "That's the worst whoopin' I've ever taken," he said, "and I don't even mind because your team played such a beautiful game."

Lindsey was now proving that she was clearly the state's best player and that Roosevelt was one of the state's best teams. Even more impressive than her stats, which filled the sports page, was how she earned them. When a team loses to the Roughriders, I want them to leave with their ego intact as much as possible, so I don't let the girls roll up the score. Once we have a dominating lead, the less-experienced players take the floor, and if they keep increasing the score, I tell them not to shoot until they've passed seven times to keep the game from turning into a massacre. With another coach, Lindsey would have rarely been subbed out and would have shattered all kinds of state records. With me, she averaged her 22.3 points per game that season in only 18 minutes.

But for months I couldn't get Lindsey to fully understand the importance of sportsmanship. She didn't pick up any opponents after knocking them down, which she did several times per game. When opponents reached in to get the ball from her, Lindsey jabbed her elbows at them. Watching Lindsey, I realized pears don't fall from an apple tree: Lindsey's family environment made her attitudes perfectly parallel to her dad's linebacker mentality.

Lindsey believed that opponents shouldn't be in her way, and when they were, they'd pay. She took no prisoners. But you must respect your opponents as well as defeat them, I tried to explain. "Nah," she said. "That's lame." I tried to convey a scenario. "What if you got knocked down and somebody tried to pick you up," I asked. Lindsey smirked. "Wouldn't happen," she said. I asked her to imagine a hypothetical situation where someone with her same name was knocked down, and the opponent tried to help that person up. I asked how that hypothetical girl would feel. "That would be humiliating," Lindsey said. "I would not allow that." I watched her face show that she understood the obvious conclusion. "And what's most humiliating," I said, "is when you help someone up . . . with a smile on your face."

Parents were amazed by her subsequent remarkable change. Even opposing coaches asked me how I got this girl with slit-your-throat intensity to be so compassionate on the court. About a month after this change in action, Lindsey approached me before practice. "You manipulated me didn't you?" she said with a humbled laugh. I told her I had no choice. "What did you expect me to do? You'd already made up your stubborn mind and I knew you were wrong. It's my job to make you and the team better in more ways than just basketball." We both laughed that it took her so long to realize my objective. "You know," Lindsey said, "you're the only coach I've had who taught me the human side, rather than just the Xs and Os."

Still, despite this change, almost every girl who played against Lindsey hated her because of her rough-and-tumble linebacker mentality. Lindsey just didn't understand why people wouldn't do everything they could at every possible moment to become the best basketball player possible. She explained this to opponents by sending them reeling with her hips, and when it came to telling her teammates she would, on occasion, use words not suitable for network television. Sometimes I doubted her pep talks would have passed most cable censors.

But Lindsey taught me that no matter how hard a girl may be on the court, the emotional needs never go away. Before her senior season began, a newspaper article said Roosevelt would go as far as Lindsey Wilson could carry them. The article caused major consternation in a team packed with talented teenagers. At practice the day the article was published, I had Lindsey lie down at center court and told all the girls to lie on top of her. "Lindsey," I said, "carry them out of the gym." Her teammates burst into laughter, and the teenage bickering was cut by that one comment.

But Lindsey left the gym and wept. I learned that as tough as this girl was, her enormous heart held an ample amount of teenage insecurity. I learned the hard way that a perfect coaching moment for someone can be a devastating moment for another.

We crushed teams that season. In the first three minutes of a game against Woodinville, we built a 16–0 lead en route to a 61–28 win. When our unbeaten record was on the line against Redmond High, Lindsey answered with 31 points in a 73–57 win. Reporters previewed our mid-season showdown with Inglemoor as one of the regular season's best games. But the beating was so bad *The Seattle Times* said the only thing Inglemoor accomplished in the first half was finding the gym. Roosevelt led 59–19 with 12 minutes to play and even though we unloaded our bench and called off our full-court press, we still won 72–41. Lindsey led all scorers with 19 points.

It had been a hard road, but Lindsey finally lost that me-against-the-world mentality. Her Roosevelt teammates no longer tired of watching her try to win games by herself. Lindsey now understood that by sharing their talents, her teammates had made her a better player. It was at this point that Lindsey realized she had a duty to share her talents as well. She also realized that her entire team—not just Lindsey Wilson—was the best in Roosevelt's history.

The highlight of the season was our game against Lake Washington. They had gone to state seven out of the previous eight seasons under coach Roger Hansen. In many ways they felt that KingCo was their league. Roosevelt was an interloper—we hadn't played any tough teams yet.

Lake Washington planned to shut down Lindsey with the quickness of guard Genea Long, who was also a star track-and-field hurdler. But one fast player wasn't enough to stop Lindsey, who scored 16 points in the first quarter. Nothing worked until Coach Hanson experimented with 6-foot-3 center Catherine Kraayveld guarding Lindsey in player-to-player defense. Catherine Kraayveld was money in every sport she played. As a soccer goalkeeper that year, she had a league-low 0.40 goals-against average. She won league track-and-field titles in javelin, discus, and shot put, and qualified for state in all three events. Her best sport was basketball, which she played professionally after being drafted by the WNBA draft in 2005. Catherine guarded Lindsey twice, and both times, Catherine held her scoreless.

At halftime, I told the team that the Kraayveld versus Wilson matchup would occur again in the second half. We could win, I said, if the other four players screened for each other and pretended to be busy setting up a play. That would leave Lindsey in the wing to go one-on-one with Catherine, and I didn't think Catherine could handle Lindsey's moves by herself.

The third quarter opened and, sure enough, there was Catherine guarding Lindsey. We scored 14 points in the third quarter—all by Lindsey, who scored almost exclusively on layins. Her Roughrider teammates executed the deception perfectly. The frustration was shown on the faces of the Lake Washington players with each spin move and set shot Lindsey nailed. But even when we had a 20-point lead, the Lake Washington Kangaroos never quit. Three of their players combined for 47 points, and with five seconds remaining, Catherine scored a layin to tie the game at 68. I called our last timeout.

"Give a screen for Lindsey," I said. "Let her get the ball. Clear out and let her pound the ball up court. She'll either score or she won't. If she scores, we win. If not, we'll beat them in overtime."

Roger told his players not to try and steal the ball from Lindsey, who had already scored 39 points. Instead, he instructed his players to stay in front of her to slow her down so she couldn't get down the court in 5.6 seconds.

One of the things that makes coaching teenagers fun is when you tell them, "Go do ABC." They'll look at you and say, "Yes, we're going to do ABC," and they're excited about ABC. Then, five seconds later you watch them do XYZ. If you ask them why they did XYZ, they never have an answer. Instead, they give you a look that says, "Why would you ask something like that?"

Roger Hansen had one of those moments in the final seconds of that game. I can imagine the mixture of agony and frustration he felt as one of his players ignored his advice and tried to steal the ball. Lindsey juked the girl, dribbled the length of our home court, pulled up just inside the arc, and nailed a 15-foot jumper as the final buzzer sounded.

The 70–68 win had a made-for-TV ending. The ball barely hit the floor before Lindsey was flooded in a sea of teammates. Parents and teenagers became of one generation as their cheers shook the wood bleachers. Reporters knew they had the perfect story—Lindsey scored 41 points to preserve our undefeated season. It was one of the best endings I've ever seen, and one I know I'll never forget. But the most moving moment of the night didn't come on the court.

"I want to say something," Lindsey said, amid the team's pandemonium that carried into the locker room. "I know it's hard on a night when one girl scores 41 points and everyone else combines for 29. I know that's rough. It's all about team, and tonight I was on. And I thank you for honoring that and letting me have a game like I did tonight."

Lindsey's school record 41-point performance was impressive, but her ability to share her talent with others was what made her and the team so powerful. I don't think she could have had a night like that if she didn't understand the importance of sharing her talents. She couldn't have scored 41 points without teammates who wanted to share their talents for her and their team, and only a player who wanted to share her skills could have given Lindsey's post-game speech. The attributes Lindsey brought to her teammates—her personality, amazing moves, humor, and an incredibly intense work ethic—came down to luck. And Lindsey learned she was lucky to inherit those traits.

Lindsey Wilson has never left our gym, because every girl who has been part of the Roosevelt program knows her story. I explain how Lindsey's work ethic led her to second-team All-American honors at Iowa State University, and a professional basketball career in Greece and Turkey. She became the most successful Roosevelt basketball graduate despite not having the height advantage and raw talent that other top players are blessed with. Instead, she garnered success by matching what innate abilities she had with nonstop drive and dedication, and then learning to share her talents. She's the model

I ask all my players to follow even though I have yet to find a player with her array of skills. I explain that Lindsey developed powerful basketball skills, but at Roosevelt, she learned that those skills are far more powerful if they are shared. And I hope Lindsey knows how lucky we were to learn from her.

Not everyone comes to the playing field with incredible talent. If you're one of the lucky ones, you have a duty to share your luck. Lindsey grew up in a vibrant, athletic family environment, worked incredibly hard, had a strong support system, and had innate athletic ability, making her an extraordinary talent. By sharing her skills, Lindsey helped create a magical team. I'm certain that Lindsey Wilson will bring an impressive array of skills to any team that is lucky enough to have her as a member.

As we ramble through life, we join numerous teams with a wide variety of goals. Each member of a team brings an assortment of skills to the table. Effective leaders attempt to mix and match these varied skills in order to solve problems and create the best team possible.

CHAPTER FOUR

Alaina Forbes

Alaina Forbes (Photograph by Casey McNerthney)

Failure Is Achieving
All Your Goals

Each season, I tell the Roughriders that failure is achieving all your goals—it means you didn't aim high enough. When you're setting goals, I explain, there's a tremendous risk that you'll aim too low. To achieve your potential, you need to be out of your comfort zone, forcing yourself to achieve things you didn't know you could do. That's how you improve.

But even in some cases when you aim exceptionally high, people may still think you failed. Alaina Forbes was one of those cases. She didn't make an all-league team. She didn't have a high point-per-game average. This girl only started one varsity game in four years. Some may consider Alaina a failure for her lack of measurable success on the Roosevelt basketball team. But in reality, she was anything but a failure. I believe Alaina was a success because she didn't settle for safe goals—her high aim propelled her to become the player many teammates credited for an undefeated regular season.

Alaina's goal was to be a varsity basketball player at Roosevelt, and though she had overwhelming odds against her, she forced herself out of her comfort zone to achieve results others didn't think were possible. She told me she kept playing basketball because our system made practices fun. She wanted her minutes, but she wanted a successful team as well. And by pursuing a starting position, she made herself and her team better. If Alaina had settled for safe goals in high school her story wouldn't be as amazing. And I don't think she would have such a strong foundation for future success.

I met Alaina when she was a sixth-grader and I was an assistant rec league coach. I can't remember any conversations that year past our introduction, and I barely remember that. The only remarkable thing about Alaina as a basketball player was how indistinguishable she was from the others. She didn't have offensive moves that others stopped to watch. She wasn't a ferocious rebounder. She never had a game with a dozen assists or a game-saving steal that friends still talk about. Off the court, she kept to herself, often speaking to peers only when spoken to.

But Alaina had something that made her unlike any other girl I've met. Something drew people to Alaina—she possessed something within her spirit that seemed almost impossible to instill in other players. Basketball was a pastime for her, and she had to have known she wasn't the star. But if she knew that, I never saw it. Every time she stepped on the hardwood, she fought like her life was on the line. She didn't have extraordinary athletic abilities, but she had the kind of hard-hat work ethic that is essential to avoid a run-of-the-mill season. You don't have to win to be successful, but I tell my players they must be dramatic. They must pursue excellence like a cheetah that has identified its prey.

Alaina was the oldest of three daughters and the product of two elementary school teachers. Her parents, Clay and Maureen, didn't want their daughters to devote their adolescent years to one activity, and Alaina embraced the opportunity. In a home commandeered by teachers, school came first, and Alaina's grades made her an honor roll staple. She was drawn to music, so she learned the trumpet. Her fall was filled by soccer, and after watching friends on the swim team, she joined that sport, too. When a position on the rec league basketball team opened up, she was there on the first day. I believe Alaina knew that the most important goal was to have fun, and I suspect that came from her dad, with whom I once witnessed a tender basketball moment.

A teammate on Alaina's seventh-grade team that I helped coach was getting hammered during a game. This girl didn't get beat once or twice—she turned the ball over every time she touched it, and opponents didn't cut her slack. Late in the game, the ball bounced into her hands. She hucked, it hit the backboard, and scored 2 points. The girl produced a grin like she'd hit the Powerball jackpot. "That's what this is all about," I said to Clay Forbes, who was standing on my right. "Absolutely," he responded. Clay realized that making people happy was better than making an impressive statistic, and I believe that mentality provided tremendous support for his daughter in basketball and in life.

Alaina was a freshman at Roosevelt in 1995, when I was in my second year as JVC coach. She made my team, and her play was just like it was on our rec league team. Alaina didn't have a shooter's touch. She wasn't issued quick-twitch defensive muscles. But she still had invaluable heart.

After the season, the Roosevelt coaches met to discuss which players would make the varsity the following year. Junior Enjoli Izidor, who was the league player of the year as a freshman and sophomore, was an obvious varsity pick. Rachel Nord, Alaina's teammate since third grade, was another shoo-in. We agreed on the role of each player, except one: Alaina.

Head coach Aileen McManus wanted to cut Alaina because she said it was clear to everyone that she wouldn't make the varsity. She was an average JVC player, Aileen said, but she wouldn't be able to handle the fast-paced, cut-throat varsity opponents. "Name someone who works harder than Alaina," I said. No coach could, because there was no such person. "She's only a sophomore," I petitioned. "Maybe something will happen and she'll become more athletic. Plus, she's going to be on my team. If there's a problem with her playing, it will be my problem." My appeal struck the generous and humane nature of Aileen, who often had a maternal stance toward her players. She agreed to keep Alaina, and we wouldn't have to break Alaina's heart after her freshman year.

Perhaps the all-time biggest upset story in sports is that of the tortoise who took down the hare. In the high school basketball world, Alaina was the Lance Armstrong of tortoises. However, little obstacles in her life continually impeded development of her basketball skills. Alaina's family spent the majority of each summer at her grandmother's beach cabin about an hour north of Seattle. I'll never be a coach that tells teenagers they can't spend time with their families, because I know how valuable a loving family like Alaina's is. The problem is, her family time took a toll on the jealous game of basketball. Every team gets better during the regular season, but it's the off-season work that engineers a state championship–caliber team.

The JVC and JV teams Alaina played for had a 52–2 record. This might lead one to the conclusion that Alaina was a winning athlete: Winning, yes. Athlete, no. When Alaina was a junior on the JV team, turmoil between the parents and coaches created an incredibly tense team atmosphere. I told Clay Forbes this after a JV game, and complained that some parents were too focused on wins and losses. That didn't make it fun for the girls and wasn't what was most important, I said. Clay reminded me of Alaina's seventh-grade teammate who had the Powerball grin after hitting the lucky shot. "You know what's important," he said. And I suspect his daughter did, too.

I became the head coach before Alaina's senior season. Before Aileen resigned as coach, she met with me to give her recommendations for the upcoming year. Aileen had a list of players that should be cut, and Alaina's name topped it. I knew why Aileen wanted to cut her, so I didn't attempt to argue.

I called Alaina in June before her senior year and asked to meet her at Roosevelt because I had news that I didn't want to deliver over the phone. She didn't seem nervous when she arrived, and I tried not to show how apprehensive I was. We took a walk around the school and I told her that only three players had made the varsity before tryouts: Lindsey Wilson, the state's best player; Devon Crosby-Helms, the heir to the throne; and Alaina. "The difference between you and the two of them," I said, "is that they'll play all the time in a close game, and you probably won't play at all." Alaina wanted to know why. "Because you're as slow as I am," I told her. "We're gonna be a crazy fast-break team, which doesn't fit your style. If we had a couple of slow, big posts there would be more time for you." If I guaranteed varsity positions to only the school's most skilled basketball players, Alaina asked, why would I keep her on the varsity? "Because your work ethic is going to make everybody better," I said.

Alaina was quiet, and appeared calm even though I thought I'd caused one of the most gut-wrenching half hours of her life. At the close of the agonizing dialogue, she asked, "Can you give me some drills that will make me quick?" The comment made me want to cry, and I'm surprised I didn't. I couldn't tell her that comments like those were exactly why she was a varsity athlete. Alaina was a girl who never relented when she set her mind to something, even when the odds against her seemed overwhelming. "Yeah, I can give you some drills," I said. "And I will. But you'll never be as quick and fast as the other guards. We're loaded at the guard position and you're only 5-foot-8. I'm not trying to hurt your feelings. I'm trying to be honest. You need to go home and rent the movie *Rudy*." The film was a favorite of Alaina's mom, and one I thought she would love. Her response was surprising and immediate. "I hate that movie," she said. I told her she'd have to get over that and understand why Rudy made Notre Dame better. "You're going to carry a big responsibility for our team next year."

Rudy also happens to be one of my all-time favorites. It's based on the true story of a blue-collar kid from Joliet, Illinois, who doesn't do well academically in high school, but dreams of playing football at Notre Dame. Through dogged and naive determination he eventually makes Notre Dame's varsity as a practice player. In one of the film's most emotional scenes, the Notre Dame starters force their coach to put Rudy in during the closing moments of the season's final game. I thought Alaina might better understand her role in the upcoming season if she took Rudy's lessons to heart.

She said later that she didn't like the movie because she didn't want to be Rudy, and she wasn't. Alaina was a different kind of hero. While Rudy went to Notre Dame to achieve his own goal, Alaina was a Roosevelt basketball player with a purpose far larger than bettering herself. She was there to inspire the team as well as to have fun. It's rare to find adults with the ability to step outside themselves for the greater good of their community. Of all the teenagers I've met, only Alaina had that ability.

When Alaina told her dad she was on the varsity team, he installed a basketball hoop at her grandmother's beach cabin, where she practiced all summer. That fall, Alaina quit playing soccer to prepare for basketball season and never missed an open gym workout. I knew Alaina acknowledged that she was guaranteed a spot on the varsity, but by the way she sprinted in a sweat-soaked jersey at tryouts, I wondered if she remembered. And though I was clear with her that she wouldn't get much playing time, her work ethic never wavered.

Other Roosevelt players who have heard me tell Alaina's story ask for specific examples of how she worked hard and I can't recall standout moments. But that's why I tell people about her. Though she never did anything dramatic, she never quit moving. When other players slacked on practicing offensive cuts, Alaina would keep charging, even though her cuts were drastically slower. I can't remember her ever complaining about conditioning drills, which some players still complain about years after graduating.

When I was unclear about a drill during practice, Alaina would ask me to explain it again. She was an honors student who would later graduate from Roosevelt with a 3.8 grade point average, so I knew her simple questions weren't for her benefit. Alaina's questions were to help her teammates, though most didn't realize how she was helping them. And though she could have pointed out my lapse in clarity more directly, she didn't because she realized the team wouldn't benefit from berating the coach. She demonstrated that her goal was to make her teammates better.

We didn't have a 6-foot girl on the roster, but still won a school record of 25 games that season, which gave Alaina more playing time than expected. But as predicted, she sat during close-scoring games. About two-thirds into the season, every girl except Alaina was offended about their playing time. Because we slaughtered teams by 30-plus points, I brought JV players up for varsity games. My goal was to keep the games close and train the JV players for future seasons. The reward for my efforts was teenage frustrations. Amanda Ostrom, a senior who was a natural mediator, was the first to tell me that players were upset about their minutes. Then I heard more about team hostility from Jade White, a senior raised on street ball, who reiterated Amanda's point with a sampler plate of four-letter expletives. They brought me back into the locker room to address the team. I knew I had to choose my words carefully.

"I'm really proud that you're gnashing your teeth about your minutes," I told the team. "I never want someone to play for me who's satisfied with their minutes, because that would mean playing time isn't important to you. So, hats off to you. But I want you to raise your hand if you work harder than Alaina." No one said a word while their eyes looked to the floor during the uncomfortable silence. "Alaina has never complained about her minutes because she's there for the team," I added.

"Raise your hand if you've outworked Lindsey Wilson in practice," I said. Alaina could have raised her hand, but that's not who she is. "Lindsey Wilson has trained herself in the off-season to be the best player in the state. She's only getting an average of 18 minutes per game because she plays for a coach who won't roll the score up. If I kept her in the whole game, as many coaches would, her statistics would be all-state. And she hasn't raised a word about it. She's also here for the team. Don't take away from yourselves. Those who are upset about your minutes, you're completely right. But think about Alaina and Lindsey, and make your own choice."

The girls told me to leave because they were going to hold an Inner Circle meeting. After the ten-minute meeting, Amanda Ostrom told me that the team understood my approach and wanted to mildly amend my substitutions. The varsity players understood why the JV players were getting minutes, and though they weren't happy about it, they would accept my plan during the regular season. But as we came closer to the playoffs, the players wanted only Alaina and the other varsity athletes playing. The Inner Circle had understood Alaina's dedication and honored her commitment.

That year, we played the Redmond Mustangs in the KingCo championship. The much-hated Mustangs tied us in the first quarter 10–10. We went on a run in the second quarter, but in the last three minutes of the first half, we may as well have gone to sleep: our commanding lead eroded to eight. I scrambled to find words to motivate the team at halftime. I knew Roosevelt was the better team. The players knew they were the better team. I'll bet even Redmond knew we had more raw talent. Our psyche was fragile and gloomy. They needed a jump start and I just plain hadn't hit a brainstorm yet.

I sat in front of the team in the locker room and was about to blurt out something when to my amazement, I heard Alaina. "Well," she said, "I hardly ever get in the game, but you guys aren't doing what we practice. If you guys do what we practice, we'd kill 'em. And I don't know why you're not doing what we practice."

It was as if we were suddenly in a vacuum and time stood still while each girl processed Alaina's crystalline, commonsense truth. Sitting amid the stone silence I knew I had just heard the only halftime speech the Roughriders needed. Alaina, who so many times knew what to say and said nothing, spoke up at the most poignant time possible. After a few seconds, the girls started screaming and jumping en mass. Alaina's message ignited the team's psyche and Redmond was about to face a raging forest fire.

Our defense held Redmond scoreless for five minutes in the fourth quarter, in which they had seven turnovers and made only three field goals. The Mustangs were left to cry over a 53–40 loss as we went home with our second consecutive league championship. And Alaina, who didn't play, won the game for us with one short speech.

Two weeks later, we beat Snohomish to earn Roosevelt's first Class 4A state berth since 1981. With Lindsey Wilson at point guard and an undefeated regular season in the bag, reporters said we were a contender for the state title. But the girls didn't buy that talk for a second. To them, the state championship trophy was ours—we just had to wait a few days to take it home.

Our first-round draw was against South Kitsap, a team that won their league championship and had a 24–2 record. If we had played like we did throughout the season, I think we would have won by 20 points. But we didn't, and with 20 seconds left in overtime we had a one-point lead. In the final seconds, South Kitsap got the ball to Natasja Allen, an all-league guard who was 12 feet out. She banked in the shot as time expired, and shattered hopes for our school's first state title with South Kitsap's 63–62 win. Alaina rode the bench as she had in every close-scoring game.

In the next day's consolation round, we faced Central Valley, a team that scored less than 50 points in all three of their pre-state losses, and we should have slaughtered them. But not one girl played like she gave a damn, which was perhaps a result of my poor coaching.

I didn't think to put Alaina in, and we lost 50–49. Alaina, who outworked everyone, didn't get a second of playing time at state and our once-undefeated season turned into one of the biggest upsets in school history. However, one of the most touching moments I've witnessed as a coach came in that somber locker room. Alaina didn't tell me how hurt she'd been, being forced to watch from the bench. But it wasn't lost on Lindsey Wilson. She sobbed in Alaina's lap not for herself, but for her teammate who didn't get to experience something every high school athlete dreams of. "I'm sorry," Lindsey told her. "I'm sorry for not playing better so you could have played."

The only game Alaina started was Senior Night, the last regular-season home game when all seniors start. We played Juanita High, and since the Rebels had never challenged us, I was able to precisely arrange when the seniors played and sat. Lindsey completely understood the value of this night and, without saying anything to anyone, made the choice to feed Alaina as often as possible. I know Lindsey could have scored 50 points if she wanted to against Juanita, but she wanted Alaina to be the star. Lindsey passed up open lanes to kick the ball to her on the wing. Every rebound Lindsey fought for was sent to Alaina. At the end of the first quarter, we were ahead 27–3, and I watched Alaina score 8 points, all on assists from Lindsey.

I knew Lindsey and her teammates understood Alaina's importance. But I didn't know what Alaina and her family thought. I wondered if she enjoyed it, if she wanted to keep going or if she did because she felt she couldn't quit.

After the win against Juanita and Alaina's career-high performance, Clay Forbes came out of the stands and approached me near the scorers table. "Thank you," he said, shaking my hand. "Thank you for the best year of Alaina's life."

Alaina was on the fringe of being cut more than any other player I've known in the Roosevelt program. The overwhelming majority of people in her shoes would have found the hurdles to becoming a varsity athlete far too daunting. But Alaina didn't back down. Her goal was to be a varsity athlete, and she aimed to better each player around her with a heart second-to-none. Alaina achieved that goal and played varsity, but she didn't stop there. She strove to become a star player on the team. And though she was far from actually becoming one, her determination and hard work ethic were personally rewarding and she proved to be a major inspiration for the team in their run to the state championships. She showed me why aiming high matters more than achieving your goals.

Defining failure as achieving all your goals is similar to saying you must take risks to succeed in life. Some of those risks don't pan out, but others make your life much better. The paths that don't work out are often part of a wonderful journey and will probably lead to a learning moment and may even have positive effects on others. If you keep choosing paths that could lead to tremendous success, one of those routes just might lead to a winning ticket.

I don't coach teenagers because I care about stats. I coach for shots like the one Alaina's seventh-grade teammate hit that gave her a Powerball-winning grin. Teammates understood Alaina's prodigious character. The Roosevelt community understood her dedication and the sacrifices she suffered to make her teammates better. That's what you remember far more than statistics. To me, that's what's really important.

CHAPTER FIVE

Angela Nefcy

Angela Nefcy (Photograph by Casey McNerthney)

Work as a Team, But Be Sure to Own Your Own Life

I t doesn't matter where you come from or who you are, you're going to hit roadblocks in your life. Some roadblocks come from bad luck. Many are unwittingly self-imposed. Some are institutional. But they're always there, and we have to overcome them. Angela Nefcy's journey through life demonstrates several types of roadblocks and how to challenge them and tip them over no matter their size.

I met Angela in 1998 when she was a ninth-grader and I was the JV coach. Fifty girls showed up for tryouts and we had to cut 11 of them. Angela couldn't shoot. She would dribble off her foot and air-ball layins. Her self-confidence was almost nonexistent. Maybe I should strike the "almost." Angela was terrible, but apparently she didn't know it. Angela showed no confidence in the outcome of any of her basketball decisions, but she loved to run and socialize with the other players. Her father had told her to turn out, but she wasn't sure if she wanted to. Angela was a paradox: she lacked self-confidence, but she wasn't troubled by its absence. No matter what went wrong during that tryout, she wore an infectious grin.

Bryan Willison, the JVC coach, wanted Angela on the team. After two days of tryouts, the head coach wanted to keep a different player, and I wanted yet another athlete. We agreed to study the three of them on the third and final day of tryouts. None of us wavered in our selections, and when tryouts were over, we fought a lengthy battle. The girl I wanted on the team was a more experienced basketball player and pretty athletic, while head coach Aileen McManus preferred a girl who was very quick and aggressive. Despite this evidential landslide, Bryan still won.

Bryan championed Angela because he liked her attitude and her defensive quickness. Angela had another thing going: she could sprint, and she could keep going forever. She made the Energizer Bunny look like a slacker. Aileen and I were skeptical, but Bryan drove his point home by reminding us that the JVC was his team and she was his first choice. We acquiesced and Angela was in—not because of her basketball ability, but because that smile of hers said we were going to have fun. It was rather remarkable that we fought so hard over the last spot on the JVC team. The decision would never affect the varsity team.

During the season, Angela was terrible on offense. I could even say she was awful. Far more often than not, Angela turned the ball over by traveling, or dribbling off her foot. Though she could figure out smart passing moves, she was reticent to make the pass, afraid she'd make a mistake. And when she did throw the pass, her toss wasn't quick or deliberate; as such the ball was often intercepted.

But as bad as Angela was on offense, her defense was close to impeccable. Sure there were things she didn't know, but the eye-bulging hustle was always there. On the other hand, a new adventure began every time she stole a pass using her keen sense of anticipation. How long before she turned the ball back over to them? The other coaches and I were often amused that Angela's course of action got her two marks in the stat book: one for the steal and one for the turnover.

At the end of Angela's freshman season, she could barely make a layin. Instead of shooting a basic layin off the backboard, she would huck the ball into the air, hitting the bottom of the rim or completely missing the backboard. On her worst days, it wouldn't have surprised me if she took a shot and missed the entire *gym*. But there was a method behind her madness—Angela purposely shot the ball incorrectly because when she did, she told herself that she didn't really miss the shot, thereby sparing her already-fragile self-esteem.

Whereas if she tried the shot correctly and missed, a tiny evil coach standing on her left shoulder would whisper, "If you hadn't tried, you'd be OK, but this way you failed." At this young age, she wouldn't deal with that reality.

I became head varsity coach the spring before Angela's sophomore year, and knew she'd never make the junior varsity because her offensive game was atrocious. That was a fact. Every Roosevelt coach agreed that she ranked 39th out of 39 players in our program. At one point, she moved to 34th—but only because five seniors graduated. As head coach, I scheduled seven practices each week during the summer and each player was required to attend at least three practices per week. Angela came to each and every practice, seven times a week, during Seattle's precious summer months. That's rare dedication from a teen.

In early July, my assistant coach asked what I would do given the intensity of Angela's workouts. We knew she'd be crushed if we let her go. We both felt that I might be creating a monster. "Sadly, I'm afraid I am going to have to cut her," I said. "It's going to make her cry. It's going to make me cry, but I have to do what's best for the team."

By summer's end, Angela's game had improved. She made layins left and right. Her free-throw percentage was up to about 70 percent and she could occasionally hit pull-up jump shots. She had basic handles, but was still unable to do spin or inside-out dribbles. I was proud of her because she dedicated her summer, practicing hard, but nevertheless, Angela had a long, long way to go to become a basketball player.

There's a monumental difference between playing basketball and being a basketball player, and most kids who try out aren't yet basketball players. A basketball player controls her territory. If she's in a crowd and receives a pass—or if she dribbles into a crowd—she knows she'll dominate that crowd. Hard-core players are goal-oriented in every aspect of every possession, while those who simply play the game lack that certain aggressive, focused drive.

Imagine a loose game ball bouncing toward the end line. Some players will just stand and watch. When I see this in practice, I often walk up to the girl who is behaving like a spectator and ask her, "How much did you pay for these seats?" On the other side of the court are true basketball players: one who sprints after the loose ball and another who kills herself sprinting until she lands in a strategic position. Once there, she owns her spot on the court, fends off the opponent, and catches the pass sent to her by the teammate who'd snagged the loose ball while diving out of bounds.

There are no explicit rules when it comes to teaching people the difference between playing basketball and being a true basketball player. As a coach, one of my most important goals is finding a route into the athletic soul of players who lack that single-minded, goal-oriented drive. I feel so fulfilled and proud when a girl once mesmerized by the bouncing of a loose game ball snaps to and becomes a focused, driven, sprinting *basketball player*. It's a wonderful transformation to witness, and to take part in. She walks off the court with a determination that she'll carry with her for the rest of her life.

For three months between summer season and tryouts, coaches are not allowed to coach, per the rules of the Washington Interscholastic Activities Association. Angela had three months to get ready for tryouts by herself. She dribbled and shot for two hours each day, five days a week for 12 weeks—60 practices on her own. Angela spent 120 hours improving her skills, with less chance of making the JV than an opposing team nicknaming Lindsey Wilson "Cuddles." By tryouts, Angela's off-season workouts had paid off and we recognized that she was now skilled enough to play on the junior varsity team. Quite simply, all that single-handed practice time infused with backbreaking passion had raised Angela's offensive game to . . . several levels above atrocious. The problem was, Angela was becoming a basketball player, but the coaches didn't foresee any realistic chance of her ever making the varsity team. And we all knew that was where she really wanted to be.

Coaches need to be honest with their players. But how do you define honesty? When I motivate players, I tell them how good they are and how good they can be in as many ways as possible. Basically, I exaggerate in an effort to ignite their teen spirit. The girls have taught me that they can blossom and explode in amazing glory when their spirits are all fired up and they believe in themselves.

Unfortunately, there is a downside: sometimes their preference of playing on the varsity transforms into an expectation. On average 20 players play basketball as freshmen, yet only three to five girls will make it to varsity. This means that, almost without fail, about 15 brokenhearted girls are forced to leave the program without ever playing varsity basketball. If I pump up a player too much, her fall is deeply disheartening. If I undersell an athlete, she may never reach her potential. I err on the side of optimism, which can, unfortunately, cause greater future heartache.

Lindsey Wilson was a senior during Angela's sophomore season. Like the Roosevelt coaches, Lindsey would often watch the JVC and JV practices while working individually on her game. She noticed potential in Angela and beat her up during water breaks and after the JV practice. Lindsey would knock her down and steal the ball from her, laughing all the while. Lindsey never stopped hammering her, and it made Angela much tougher. An outsider might have claimed unusual cruelty, but that was not Lindsey's intention. Lindsey felt she had the opportunity to leave a legacy. She was molding Angela into a future varsity player by treating her like an opponent. Lindsey knew that if Angela was challenged as often as possible, she'd have an easier time handling the confrontations of a varsity game.

One day after practice, I found Angela repeatedly throwing a basketball at the wall to vent her frustration. I joked with her about what a great teammate the wall was because it always shot the ball back to her. She looked at me like I was insane.

Perhaps her instincts about me were accurate, but I was trying to ease the tension and find out what was bugging her. Eventually, she explained how Lindsey's constant harassment was making her angry. I asked Angela whether she knew if Lindsey was harassing anyone else in the program. She told me, "No, just me." So, attempting to get Angela to realize what was obvious to me, I asked her why she thought Lindsey was singling her out.

Angela's baffled face made it seem as though I'd handed her a Rubik's Cube and asked her to solve it in less than a minute. I let her flounder for a while, and when my prompting didn't help her realize what Lindsey was doing, I asked Angela if it was possible that Lindsey was tough only on her because she wanted her to succeed. Was it possible that Lindsey was treating Angela the same way she treated her varsity teammates? I told her to think about the idea that she was being singled out by the best player in the state. Could it be because she saw great potential in Angela?

That year, Angela's junior varsity play was ordinary and unremarkable. She didn't have Lindsey Wilson's throat-slitting aggression, and didn't stand out among competitors. She wasn't bad, nor was she good—but she did have her shining moments. In a JV game against Rogers High, we were trailing by 3 points with nine seconds to go. We shot a 3-pointer, Angela pulled down the rebound, and dribbled backwards to drain a three at the buzzer. We went on to win the game in overtime. But Angela didn't feel like the hero. Her dad told me that on the drive home all she talked about was how she screwed up in the first half and how the game never would have been close if she'd done well then. Angela didn't think she was heroic because she really was only in a position to lose the game. If she missed the shot, she would have let her teammates down. So there was no question that she had to make that 3-pointer, and to Angela, that didn't make her a hero. She didn't believe she'd had an ESPN moment—that she'd hit that shot because of her talent. She thought she'd hit it to avoid the out-and-out personal disaster of letting her teammates down. Angela could only focus on the negative aspects of her game, and she couldn't see that perhaps it was her skills, not luck, that drove that ball into the hoop.

Later that year, the JV coach couldn't attend a game against Redmond High, so I acted as coach for both the varsity and JV. As the fourth quarter wound down, we were up by about 8 points and needed defense. I told Angela to get in the game. What did Angela do? She refused. She told me I was wrong; she wasn't good enough and shouldn't be put in at such a crucial moment. "Angela, get in the game and kick their ass!" I said, and forced her in. The first pass shot to Angela went through her fingers out of bounds in front of our bench. "See?" she said, looking back at me. "I was right." But after about a minute, Angela's nerves settled as I hoped they would and her animalistic defense helped get the stops we needed. Roosevelt won the game primarily because of her amazing late-game defense.

The summer between Angela's sophomore and junior years, I increased weekly practices to eight and required players to attend at least four per week. Once again, Angela showed dogged determination to improve her game by attending practice eight times a week. By the end of that summer, she could make free throws at about an 80 percent clip, with her eyes closed. She developed handles. She had the purest shooting form in the program. There was only one person who didn't realize that: Angela.

She made the JV again as a junior. We knew she'd really hoped to make varsity for her junior year, but despite all her hard work her skills still weren't up to par. Relegated once again to JV and with full knowledge that there were freshman players on the varsity team, Angela hung in there and remained loyal to the program. A more egocentric teen would have tossed in the towel and stomped off the court never to be seen again.

During the first month of the season, we decided to bring some JV players to the varsity practice to see how they performed, and to let them get used to how fast and how violent the big show really was. The plan was to rotate a couple different JV players up each week. After the first week, my assistant coach thought Angela played well enough to earn a second week. There wasn't one specific thing she did well, but the assistant coach was convinced that she practiced like a true *basketball player*. I wasn't certain of that, but acquiesced. By the second week, Angela's spirit and skills proved that she could be a full-on varsity player.

"Congratulate Angela," I told the team in the locker room after practice. "We're promoting her to the varsity." Her new varsity teammates shook the room with cheers and swarmed her with high-fives and handshakes. Angela went home and told her dad, "I don't know what happened, but everyone was giving me high-fives and I can't figure out why." Her dad called me to find out what happened. We realized that when I made the announcement, Angela was in such disbelief that she couldn't even process that she made the varsity team. This type of hard-earned achievement wasn't in her field of vision, and her ghost-like self-esteem buried the truth: she was so good that she'd been elevated to the next level.

She played in her first varsity game against Redmond, one of our chief rivals. I've never seen a girl who wasn't scared entering her first varsity game. In Angela's case, she wasn't just scared, she was terrified as she subbed in during the third quarter. The way her eyes scanned the crowd as she went to the scorers table to check in, she showed that she lacked the proper focus for competition. She was starting to get her rhythm after a few possessions when a Redmond girl blindsided her, sending her careening into the bleachers. It's a rivalry game, and players in any good rivalry are capable of that. You can tell your girls until you're blue in the face that sportsmanship is paramount, but in the end they're still going to hammer their rivals. Later in the third, Meghan Miller, one of our take-no-prisoners, Charles Barkley kind of players leveled the Redmond player who'd slammed Angela. Meghan bashed her when she ran through the key, and laid her out flat. The dazed opponent lay there, knowing she played for Redmond, but not much else. Angela was stunned, her mouth hung agape. Meghan winked at her. "That's when I really knew I was on the varsity," Angela told me later, beaming.

Between her junior and senior years, Angela wanted more from the summer workouts that she never missed. "I don't want a high school practice," she announced at a spring meeting. "I want a *college* workout." With one more year until she graduated from Roosevelt, Angela knew she wasn't going to play college ball, but she wanted to make the team better. Angela knew that I demanded from each player as much as she could give. She knew I tried to push girls past the place where they thought they could go. Each girl was being asked to bend to the will of the team. In some way Angela reasoned that the will of the team was something bigger than what her teammates saw. Bending to the will of the team includes sacrificing to better yourself. She practiced speed dribbling, hesitation dribbling, free throws, spin dribbles, pull-up jumpers—insisting that all drills be done at break-neck speed. During her 120-minute workouts, Angela took only four water breaks that lasted two minutes each.

One of my best-loved moments occurred the summer between Angela's junior and senior years, when Roosevelt played a game against Juanita High—a team we usually beat by an average of 30 points. The Roughriders taught a hoop camp for elementary school kids during the day, and by game time they were exhausted. At halftime, Roosevelt trailed Juanita by 19 points. "This is summer," I said. "It doesn't matter who wins the game, but this will be the first time ever that Roosevelt lost to Juanita High School. If that's OK with you, that's OK with me because it's your team. On the other hand, you played really poorly and without much heart. All I'm going to remember is how hard you play in the second half. We've already lost the game and it doesn't matter. This is your issue, not my issue. I want you to figure out how you're going to play well in the second half. I have a long memory and I won't forget if you don't go all out in the second half."

I stormed out, convinced I'd given one of the all-time best half-time speeches. I let them know I was disappointed but I'd also let them off the hook in a sense. I was giving them the chance to step up to the baseline and own their own territory. As I entered the gym, I started to laugh. There they were, trying their best to deal with what I'd said, and yet, I didn't care whether we won or lost. What is important is the fact that they're out there trying, with my words ringing in their ears. That's all that mattered—that they'd listened, processed, and would carry that with them into life, which is a better "win" than the fleeting moment of winning a game. In the second half, the girls went crazy. Angela nabbed seven steals in the third quarter, and on the seventh, a teammate stopped on the court, put her hand on her hip and gazed at the magnificence of Angela's performance. Halfway through the fourth quarter, *we* were up by 19 points. At that point, Angela's dad, Chris, entered the gym. Unaware we'd just made an incredible comeback, Chris said, "Looks like another Roosevelt blowout over Juanita, as usual."

Later that night, Chris told me what Angela had said to the team at halftime, after I'd delivered my Captain Guilt Trip speech and stomped out of the locker room. "Bill leaves, and they're all looking at me," Angela confessed to her dad. "I realized I'm the only senior. I'm the one that has to lead them, and I've never done this. I don't *want* to do this. So I said, 'OK, let's agree on one thing: Bill's a jack-ass.' And they agreed in unison, 'Yeah, Bill's a jackass.' 'And you know what that jackass will do? If we lose this game, we will never stop hearing about it. He'll bring it up all season long. He'll probably mention it at our wedding receptions. The only way to shut him up is to go out and beat Juanita. Then we don't have to deal with the jackass anymore.' And we all agreed that's what we'd do." It wasn't my halftime speech that had done the trick—the incredible comeback was due to Angela Nefcy's taking the helm as team leader, for her very first time.

Angela finally got into her groove as a senior. She knew her role, was more vocal, and didn't hesitate in drills as she did the three previous years. During the first practice after tryouts, she passed on a wide-open 3-pointer. Why? Because Angela believed that everybody on the team was a better shooter than her. She was wrong, but that's what she believed. When she passed on the open shot, I made the entire team run a Sweet 16. "I knew he'd make me run if I passed up a shot, and that's no problem because I can run forever," she told her dad after practice. "But I never thought he'd make the *whole team* run on account of my actions." Angela's dad, Chris, played on Brother Rice High's 1974 team, which won the school's first Michigan state basketball championship. Chris, who exuded enormous self-confidence, knew Angela didn't share that trait. Chris beamed when he recalled Angela's reaction, because he understood I was forcing his daughter to believe in herself. We both knew the most important skill to develop was Angela's self-confidence.

Angela hit some major roadblocks her senior year, which began when she collided with a teammate during practice, bruising her right hand so badly that she couldn't play or practice for two weeks. When her hand recovered, she caught a bronchial virus and was out another three weeks of the regular season. Her senior season was wasted, but she was finally healthy and rejoined the team as we entered the playoffs.

During the district championship against Redmond, opponent Ashley Graham went on a hot streak against Darnellia Russell, our star guard, scoring 9 points in the first two and a half minutes. Graham was the league's top scorer, and Darnellia should have known better. "Angela, sub in for Darnellia," I said. She sat down next to me and said, "Oh, no, no, no. I can't go in for Darnellia. She's the best player in the state. You're wrong. I can't go in."

"Shut up and listen," I said. "This is what's going to happen: if Ashley gets a shot off the rest of the game, you'll have no idea how disappointed I'll be." In truth, if Ashley had continued to shoot as she had, the game would have been a blowout. I pressed Angela into the game, and when she went in, she was possessed. Angela flew around the court and smothered Graham before she had the ball. When Graham got it, Angela was so deep in her grill that there was no way Ashley could fire off a reasonable shot. But more incredibly, when openings appeared Angela actually shot, which was a complete change of behavior. When the dust settled, Angela had scored a career-high 8 points. Graham had none. The only shot she got off was an NBA-range 3-pointer—a frustration huck that didn't even come close to the basket. In the locker room, I gave Angela the game ball for winning the bi-district championship. Her teammates erupted— they all agreed she deserved it. It was one of the all-time feel good moments in my coaching career. Angela had made tremendous progress. Instead of being cut after her freshman year, Angela had become the team leader. She had learned to better herself and still do what had to be done for the team.

About three hours later, Angela's dad called and wanted to talk. When we met, he told me how Angela cried the entire way home after the district championship against Redmond. In Angela's mind, it didn't matter that the only shot Graham was able to manage didn't have a prayer of going in. Angela thought she failed her mission. My instructions were "She takes no shots." Graham took a shot, ergo, mission catastrophe. What Angela didn't see was the bigger picture: without her, we wouldn't have won the bi-district championship. But it wasn't as much a self-esteem problem as it was an issue of focus. Angela had transformed into a player who, given a goal, wasn't satisfied unless she achieved it, completely and absolutely.

After high school, Angela enrolled at Western Washington University and I pounced on the opportunity to offer her future life lessons. Halfway through her first quarter, I bet her that she would get a 3.1 or higher grade point average because knowing Angela Nefcy, I knew she would bet against herself. The "wager" was $3,000 and she, of course, lost the bet because she did better than she expected. Instead of collecting, we continued the bet each quarter, double or nothing. Each quarter we increased the threshold GPA. "I'm not betting with you anymore," Angela said, days before returning to Western for the final quarter of her junior year. "You're an old man and you know tricks that I can't figure out." I smiled, as she "owed" me $24,000 at the end of her sophomore year. Angela hadn't won a single bet, and her GPA had blossomed to 3.86.

I told her that was fine. She was a chicken, and I didn't expect that to change. "OK," she said, giving in to my taunting. "I bet I won't get a 4.0." That statement made me as nervous as Angela was in her first varsity game. It was possible that I'd lose my double-or-nothing bet. $24,000 of bragging rights would be gone. We shook hands.

Throughout the quarter, Angela's dad fed me insider information about her performance in each class. She'd aced her first four midterms, but hadn't yet taken the hardest one. She called her dad after her final midterm to tell him she'd bombed it. It was the perfect time to weasel out of the bet. Before I could manipulate her, Angela got her score. She aced it. "Angela, have you ever thought about intentionally getting a B so you can finally win a bet?" I asked when she was home for a weekend. She responded with an evil laugh. Five weeks of complete uncertainty followed. We had no way to check Angela's grades other than her verbal statements, which weren't completely trustworthy. When she showed her final grades to her dad and me, suddenly I was $24,000 richer. Angela had earned a perfect 4.0. I'm happy to report that I'm the only person in the world who can turn the achievement of a perfect 4.0 into a sad event.

Angela bet against herself every time we wagered in her freshman, sophomore, and junior years of college. Her worst GPA was a 3.38 the fall of her junior year, but she'd taken difficult courses—courses I'd never dreamed of attempting as an underclassman. During the spring of her freshman year, when most Western students risked missing fascinating lectures by sprawling on the lawn in front of Old Main, Angela earned a 3.5. That summer, she recorded a 3.75 and followed with a 3.9 and 4.0 in her next two quarters. I knew only one person who would bet against herself with a record like that.

I taunted Angela: "There will only be one more bet. Then I'll have enough to buy a Lexus with all the trimmings." If I had kept my mouth shut, she probably wouldn't have bet again. But where's the fun in that? Angela refused to make bets after my Lexus barb. But I couldn't give up. There had to be a way to keep the bet going. Chris and I went over strategies, and after a month, I made my move.

"How about one of us comes up with a grade point average and the other person bets over or under," I suggested, even though Angela was three weeks into winter quarter. We'd made most of our bets after the quarter had started, but Angela still bet against herself. She accepted my offer and after much consternation, decided to let me pick the GPA. I chose 3.85. It took her two weeks to decide whether to bet over or under my chosen GPA. The quarter was wearing on and she was racking up more and more data points. For the first time in her life, Angela had bet on herself, saying that she would get a GPA higher than 3.85.

Her dad had supplied me enough information to know I would lose the double-or-nothing bet. To give Angela another chance to bet on herself, I offered her two choices: she could settle for a small amount of money instead of risking a major loss, or we could increase the bet. If Angela took the second option and won, I would owe her $36,000 instead of nothing, but I joked that only a miracle would put her above a 3.85 to make that happen. To win money, Angela would have to overcome her self-confidence issues.

Angela called me about two weeks before the quarter was over. "I'm betting on myself this time." I asked if she was sure she wanted to do that, and then thanked her for the decision. I was looking forward to my new car's soft and supple leather interior. "Wait! I don't know what to do," Angela said, somewhat panicked. "I don't know what to do." I stuck to my guns. "Bet on yourself," I insisted. "Trust me, I can use the Lexus. What color would you recommend?" Angela hung up, stuck between believing in herself and helping me win a dream car.

She graduated from Western with an overall GPA of 3.76 and a degree in manufacturing supply chain management. By the way, I appreciate you buying this book—I still owe Angela Nefcy $36,000.

After graduation, Angela received multiple job offers and chose to work at Microsoft, where her bosses have recognized her as a strong young leader. She has developed a sense of self-confidence that allows her to be someone management turns to when they need to solve problems. As she had for the Roosevelt Roughriders, I believe she will continue to work hard for what's best for her Microsoft team.

Angela went from a girl who was afraid to shoot a layin to a successful businesswoman. After all those obstacles in her life, she now faces the world in the driver's seat. Her spirit taught much more than I could ever teach her.

Molly Boyd

Molly Boyd (Photograph courtesy Gilbert W. Arias/Seattle Post-Intelligencer)

CHAPTER SIX

Molly Boyd

*Molly Boyd (Photograph courtesy Gilbert W. Arias/*Seattle Post-Intelligencer*)*

You Can't Have a Championship Team Without Sacrifice

I n my fifth year as Roughrider head coach, the team won the Class 4A state championship for the first time in Roosevelt school history. Almost all conversations about the Roughriders that last more than five minutes include questions about how we won that title with a team that some fans didn't think would even make the tournament. What was the secret to your coaching? How did you run practices? What off-season workouts did you require for your players? Honestly, there are no secrets to my coaching. The practices during the playoffs comprise the same drills we do all season, but they are 30 minutes shorter. We might design one new quick-hitter scheme on offense so we have something that opponents haven't seen in game film. Off-season can always be summed up with two words: hard work.

When you get to the state tournament, every team is talented— so talented that any of the 16 teams can hoist the championship trophy high above their heads and haul it back to their campus trophy case. To win, you need a combination of spirit and luck. You can't be a championship team without sacrifice, and you can't be a championship team without someone like Molly Boyd.

Molly, a 5-foot-9 guard, was not a standout athlete at Roosevelt. Molly loved country music, and often came to practice with several pairs of outrageous sunglasses. She wasn't afraid to call people out for their actions, but wouldn't be the person standing in front of the team giving a speech. Molly led with the kind of contagious laughter that would make even Oscar the Grouch crack a smile. Her only sibling was her younger sister, but both Molly and her sister Megan considered many of their basketball teammates siblings. As a freshman, she was hesitant to challenge teammates in practice, which limited her to the junior varsity team. But she was the most skilled at establishing friendships, forming vibrant, cohesive groups at practices. It wasn't that Molly always needed to be with others. The converse was true— one or more of her teammates always wanted to be around Molly.

There were no juniors Molly's sophomore year in 2004, so we promoted her ahead of schedule along with several sophomore teammates. Molly made the varsity in the sense that her name adorned the gym's green-and-gold varsity readerboard, but she wasn't truly a varsity athlete. Her 5-foot-9 frame made her a "tweener"—a nickname for players that are a little bit guard and a little bit post. She wasn't quick enough to defend true guards and she wasn't big enough to hammer posts. Because she was tentative, almost all loose balls and rebounds near her belonged to the opponents. She panicked with the ball, like she'd been given a grenade that was about to explode. Like a starving tiger on the hunt, Molly gave herself to the game 100 percent, but she wasn't issued quick-twitch muscles. She played limited minutes in nine varsity contests, scoring 11 total points. The overwhelming bulk of her experience was in junior varsity games. Alas, Molly didn't have the quickness required to be a standout athlete in an elite program. But which is more important: athleticism or heart?

We lost our opening game that state championship season because our star player, Darnellia Russell, was declared ineligible by the Washington Interscholastic Activities Association and Tracy Leddo, a 5-foot-4 senior guard who averaged 9.5 points per game, was injured. When Darnellia and Tracy returned to team play, Roosevelt crushed Kent-Meridian High, a feared South Puget Sound

League opponent, 73–45. No one on the team saw this as unexpected. Roosevelt was full of athletes and carried the kind of swagger that showed they had no plans to be beaten. After a holiday festival, we won four games to extend our win streak to 11. In our locker room after tenacious beatings, there was no discussion of how we pounded opponents like a middle school bully. The team displayed an air that showed they expected to wipe the floor with opponents, and never once thought they were second best.

During this run, Molly only played in blowouts, scoring a mere 5 points in our 11-game win streak. In practice, her game improved because she practiced dribbling, passing, and shooting drills like a machine without an off switch. Molly understood why most drills conclude with a winner and a loser, and when she acted on that understanding, increased aggression followed. She yelled random statements that were almost always completely out of any known context, but her teammates loved it because she spiced up monotonous practices. The intelligence that put her on Roosevelt's honor roll also pushed her to become an astute help- and weak-side defender. Wherever the ball is becomes the *strong side*. The *weak side* is the other half of the court. Defenders on the weak side must overcome a natural tendency to guard their girl. They must rotate away from her toward the ball. Some high school girls never understand this concept. Molly, though, became quite good at it.

However, in both JV and varsity games, I thought Molly played like a month-old kitten at the Westminster Dog Show. But there was something about Molly, something about the way she barked encouragement to her teammates, that made her the emotional lynchpin of the 2004 team.

My coaching style allows lots of players to get in the action. Most other coaches play the same eight players—and only those eight—in order to ensure that one of the best players is on the court at all times. Those coaches are there to win: and only to win. It's not unusual for me to play 13 or 14 different girls during a game because I try to reward players for the effort they gave during the week's practices. If we lose because of it, well, that's my problem. And trust me, I get an earful when we do. The only drawback is that when underclassmen get a taste of varsity minutes, they typically want more. But in general I don't give underclassmen more than about three or four minutes in varsity games, which frustrates those players and their parents. What they don't realize is that underclassmen at most other schools don't get to play at all. In Molly's case, if I anticipated a close finish, she wouldn't play until I knew our victory was secured. I'd put her in for a couple minutes at the end of the game, while other JV players whom I considered more athletic were getting four minutes. Molly, like any competitor stuck in this position, wanted to play more.

Nine weeks into the season, Roosevelt put its 11-game winning streak on the line against Garfield High, a cross-town rival and the state's top-ranked 4A team. The Garfield Bulldogs were feared by schools across the state, but not by the Roughriders, who had a 6 p.m. tip-off. The day before the game, Molly was full of ideas as we planned the usual pre-game shoot-around. Shoot-arounds are held a few hours before game time, when we gather in the gym and casually take a hundred or so game-style shots. A shoot-around's main benefit isn't to practice—it's designed to calm teenage nerves that can and will bounce off the gym walls if left unmanaged. We walk through our defenses and kick around our game strategy that we've tailored for the team we'll face later that day. After the hour-long shoot-around, players planned to take a pre-game nap, wake up with an hour or so to gossip via text messaging, eat a snack, and then go down to send the Bulldogs home howling with their tails between their legs. Because Molly had the pre-Garfield shoot-around detailed to the minute, she determined that it had to start at 11 a.m. to fit the day's schedule. All agreed.

Molly's schedule would have been as smooth as the shoot-around had I not received a frantic call from the Roosevelt boys basketball coach, telling me that all the games had been moved up two hours to 4 p.m. Our athletic director was aware of the change for a week, but she forgot to tell any of the basketball coaches. At times like that, I felt the athletic director was lucky there were laws prohibiting murder.

In a panic, I hit the phones like a lone police station switchboard operator during a downtown shooting rampage. My assistant coaches and I started calling players just after 2 p.m., trying to wake them from their naps with enough time to get to the south Seattle gym. The girls straggled into the Bulldog gym between 3:15 and 3:45 p.m. Warm-ups felt like *Night of the Living Dead*, except these zombies weren't as scary. In our huddle I tried to get the girls angry at the athletic director, searching desperately for a spark to ignite that precious teenage spirit. "Let's not let the AD ruin our day," I shouted. "Let's kick Garfield's ass and beat them and our athletic director. We're going to *win* in this scenario." The team was too tired and irritated to care. Though I told no one, I knew by their body language that we were going to get spanked. It's no fun being around 12 teenage girls who've been woken prematurely to the news that their entire schedules were rearranged due to someone else's error.

I was wrong. We didn't get spanked. We got horse-whooped, by 21 points. Rare was the play that a Garfield girl didn't talk trash. Our opponent accentuated each basket they scored and each steal they made with an exaggerated shriek. Garfield's coach, Joyce Walker, strutted up and down the sidelines like a peacock. Joyce graduated from Garfield in 1980, and later became a two-time All-American at Louisiana State University, averaging nearly 25 points per game. She was the second female to join the Harlem Globetrotters, and is a member of the Washington Interscholastic Athletic Association Hall of Fame. Many coaches believe that Joyce is Washington's all-time best female basketball player. That night, outsiders thought that her team was one of the best in state history, too. We were humiliated by the punishing loss. Heads down, we sulked into our locker room. This once proud, unbeatable basketball team had been transformed into leftover Hamburger Helper.

I'm sorry to say that I have been in many locker rooms after big losses. It takes at least five minutes for the crying to settle down enough for me to attempt bolstering their spirits and slipping in a few life lessons. Throughout my so-called words of post-game wisdom that evening, sniffles filled the room. But after such a pounding, I was surprised that not one tear was shed. I swear the room was so dry it would have been a mistake to strike a match. Only one emotion permeated that room: anger. And only one player spoke. "I'm not mad at our athletic director," Molly said. "I think we should thank her. Garfield thinks that we're no good. Does anyone in this room think that Roosevelt came to this game today? I hate to lose, but this isn't going to hurt us. The next time we play them, they'll be completely surprised." Molly was right—Roosevelt had played like an entirely different team that game, but Joyce and the Bulldogs didn't know that.

As Molly's words sank into her teammates' psyches, the mood in the locker room changed from cold-steel anger to near elation. Within a minute, sullen faces and tight-grim mouths were replaced with animated conversations spiked with laughter. By the time the team left the locker room, the players displayed a knockout self-confidence that would make outsiders think we were undefeated. To this day, though, I still wrestle with who was really responsible for our loss that evening: Garfield or our athletic director.

Roosevelt won its next game by 33 points. We entered the playoffs with an 18–2 record, riding a seven-game win streak in which we beat teams by a 20-point average. After the final regular season game, I went to celebrate at The Duchess, a Roosevelt bar and social club, with several of the parents and assistant coaches. We talked about how the players had progressed, and how the team had rallied back from the fluke loss to Garfield. We replayed the wins against Lake Washington and the much-hated Redmond Mustangs. Any time we beat Redmond, we relive that victory until the next time we turn the Mustangs into Big Macs. Recalling stories from those games never gets old. But that evening, there were no standout stories of how Molly played during the regular-season-ending win streak. She'd only scored 2 points in the final seven games.

As we reminisced at The Duchess, I mentioned to an old fraternity brother that I thought we could beat Garfield to win the school's fifth KingCo 4A championship and earn one of the league's two state tournament berths. He looked at me like I was wearing a uniform from a mental institution I'd just escaped from. "Resler, you're not going to state," he said. "You're such an eternal optimist." In my mind, I knew it was possible. All I told him was, "We have a good team." I guess I didn't downplay my optimism enough. He still showered me with belittling laughter, treating me like a dumb kid with a great baseball card collection.

My friend didn't take into account that we were 4–0 in title games, winning KingCo 4A league titles in 1998, 1999, 2001, and 2002. Our only loss besides the season opener was the fluke loss to Garfield, a team we would face in the upcoming KingCo championship. The Bulldogs' only losses were their non-league season opener and a 53–52 mid-season upset to Redmond. Our seven-game win streak paled in comparison to their impressive 14-game sweep.

In the pre-game locker room before the KingCo championship, the girls brought their "bring on Garfield" attitude. They couldn't wait for the game to start because they knew they were about to reveal the surprise Molly had portended in her locker room speech after the fluke loss. That night, Garfield would meet an entirely different team compared to the last time they'd played Roosevelt. Our warm-ups looked like war time; Garfield's pre-game looked like party time. The first quarter matched two of the state's best teams in a compellingly close, on-the-edge-of-your-seat game. If it been broadcast, it might have gotten higher ratings than the WNBA finals. In the second quarter, I could feel the momentum swinging our way. Both teams played an in-your-grill, rugged defense on 84 feet of hardwood. Anywhere a fan looked, they'd see face-to-face, in-your-eye confrontations. When we took a 1-point lead into halftime, the bleachers rocked like a Pearl Jam concert.

We owned Garfield in the third quarter. After five minutes, they had managed only one bucket. We led 35–25 with 3:17 remaining in the third quarter, playing a 2–3 zone defense that put the Bulldogs on a leash. At the start of the fourth quarter, we were ahead 38–30. We only needed a few points to hold on. Instead, we had turnovers on our first four possessions. On the fifth and sixth, we improved: we fired air balls. We didn't score in the fourth quarter until 3:43 remained, when Tracy Leddo hit a free throw. The remaining few minutes weren't much better, as we scored a whopping 3 points. Late in the fourth, Garfield forward Samantha Tinned, who would later become the two-time state tournament MVP, hit a five-footer in the lane, cutting our lead to 39–37.

With just 13 seconds remaining, we were up by a single point. In the previous day's workout, we had spent significant time practicing that exact scenario. We'd practiced passing up all shots except uncontested layins. When the ball was inbounded, the girls were coached to run out the clock. Darnellia Russell took the inbounded ball, then did her own thing—she broke open for a reverse layin. Darnellia had the whole court in front of her to run out the clock. Instead, she took the shot. There are only two girls in the history of Roosevelt basketball who would make the shot 999 times out of 1,000: Lindsey Wilson and Darnellia Russell. Unfortunately, it wasn't Darnellia's lucky night.

Garfield snagged the rebound and somehow, some way, some ethereal being reached down and convinced one of my girls to foul Malia O'Neal, Garfield's 5-foot-6 all-league guard who then sank one of two free throws with 11.3 seconds, sending the game into overtime. Darnellia answered by scoring 5 points of her game-high 16, hitting a 3-pointer to regain our lead with 2:40 remaining in overtime. Then Mackenzie Argens, our 6-foot-2 freshman, fouled out. This left us a good bit short—literally. Garfield now had the advantage, with three players who towered over our tallest available player. Garfield went on a 5–0 run in the final 2:18, and we lost the KingCo championship 50–46.

Our Mackenzie Argens had controlled Garfield forward Samantha Tinned throughout the game. Luckily, this was lost upon

Garfield's coach, and she wouldn't make the needed adjustment for Mackenzie in the future. "I thought we only played four minutes of basketball," Joyce Walker told the *Seattle Post-Intelligencer*, referring to the overtime period. "They were the most important four minutes and we were really fortunate." Tinned, who was scoreless in the first half, scored 4 points of her team-high 13 in overtime.

Again, Molly watched the entire game from the bench. Throughout this playoff roller coaster, a heartbreaking scenario lurked in the wings. KingCo 4A playoff rules allowed 15 girls to suit up for playoff games, while the Washington Interscholastic Activities Association, which governed the state championship, allowed only 12.

If we qualified for state, I would have to tell three players that they'd be on the bench watching their teammates when we performed on the state's biggest stage. Deciding which girls would hear this awful message was as unclear as the 2000 presidential election.

One of the hardest decisions a coach must make is when to give a team information that could affect the players or the team. Suppose I had told the three not suiting up before the playoffs began. Those girls would be devastated to the point that they may not even practice well, which might affect other players. And if we didn't make it to state, that heartache would be for no reason at all. I knew that once I delivered the news of who wouldn't be in the state championship, it would spread through the team like wildfire. Sides would be taken and high school drama would abound.

I always worry that this type of announcement will destroy my team's performance and hurt their chances at qualifying, and that my premature action won't produce anything positive for the girls or their families. The other option is to withhold the information. If the team doesn't qualify for state, no one has hurt feelings. If we do qualify for state, only then do I have to come forward. In this case, the three girls who are cut get hurt.

There is a drawback to this approach. Three players who would revel in the whipped-cream-pies-in-the-face celebration if we did qualify would face unbelievable dismay the following day when told they wouldn't suit up at state. Those three players feel more paralyzing pain than if I'd told them before the playoffs. It's a lousy tradeoff, and in this case one that I wrestled with for several weeks.

We'd lost that KingCo 4A championship to Garfield, and the only way we could make it to state was by beating the much-hated Redmond Mustangs. If we beat those entitled Eastside rivals, a raucous celebration would have ensued. But, unbeknownst to Molly, a victory against Redmond would cause her to suffer her own personal train wreck.

We faced Redmond in a neutral gym. The first quarter ended with Redmond ahead 11–2. On every basket the Redmond fans, players, and coaches behaved as though they'd won the universe championship: jumping out of chairs, frenetic screaming, taunting Roosevelt players, whom they respected as much as meter maids. Two minutes later, 11–2 looked pretty good as Redmond poured in 5 unanswered points. I thought it was over at 16–2. All I wanted was to get out of the game with the girls feeling better about life. Winning may have been out of the question, but life lessons are never off the menu. Then we blew through their defense and sank a layin. Redmond called a timeout.

Roosevelt was emotional, and I knew the wrong words would crush them. The coaches searched for delicate words to inspire the team. My mind was cluttered as I entered the team huddle hoping one of my ideas would work. I was about to speak when Darnellia launched a string of expletives that made John McEnroe seem like June Cleaver. You'd never know we were trailing 16–4 by the body language exhibited in that huddle. Darnellia continued, "We scored and they had to call a timeout! They're scared and we own them!" Throughout Darnellia's firebrand speech, Molly nodded her head. Another rich stream of opprobrious language from Darnellia made it clear that I should back away. The Inner Circle was immediately in session.

The Roughriders outscored the Mustangs 17–10 in the second quarter and beat them 9–6 in the third. We were ahead in the final minute, but knew the game would be determined by a last-second shot as Redmond inbounded the ball with 12 seconds remaining. With three seconds on the clock, Redmond all-league guard Mackenzie Flynn sent a pass toward teammate Claire Pallansch that could have given the Mustangs a chance to earn their sixth consecutive state berth. But Roosevelt freshman Ariel Evans cut across the key and caught it, chest-high. Roosevelt won 42–41, qualifying us for the state tournament.

After we qualified, each Roosevelt coach helped me analyze players' physical skills and the emotional toughness they brought the team. We analyzed who we wanted on the floor in each scenario, and who we'd substitute in each situation. There would be four games over four days at the state tournament, and fatigue would plague us. Playing back-to-back games leaves you feeling like you were in a head-on car wreck: everything aches.

After two painful weeks of deliberations, the coaches decided to fill the two final spots with freshmen Allison Reiman and Colleen Bresee. Molly, a sophomore, did not make the state cut. The freshmen had played fewer varsity minutes combined than Molly did alone, but had become better players over the course of the season. In half the minutes of varsity play, they'd outscored Molly 42–11. But what impressed me most was their quicker juke moves. Allison and Colleen were better dribblers, better passers. They didn't adapt quickly to practice drills—freshmen rarely do—but they were less hesitant to take action than Molly. The decision was close, and in my opinion, any decision could have been right.

When it was time to break the news to the girls who hadn't made the cut, the last girl I met with was Molly. "I have something to say that is extremely difficult, but I have no choice, and I feel bad," I told her. "I've decided that we need to have Allison Reiman and Colleen Bresee to complete the state team." Molly looked me in the eye and nodded. "And I want you on the bench. I need you there. But you're not going to be one of the 12 that suits up." She showed no emotion, making eye contact and nodding. "Yeah," she said. "OK." As she left the gym I turned to my assistant coach, Bryan Willison. "I think she took it pretty well."

Driving home, my cell phone rang and displayed Molly Boyd's home number. When I answered, Molly's mom seemed panicked. "You have to come over immediately," Jennifer Boyd demanded. She didn't say much else and based on her voice, I assumed the worst. I knew that Molly might be seriously hurt from the news. As I turned my car around, I prepared for a nightmare.

I felt like a weary old barn about to be hit by the emotional tornado I'd churned up. I knew my decision had injured one of the most exquisite souls I'll ever know, and I had a doomsday anticipation as I headed up the Boyds' walkway. The only thing between me and disaster was their front door, and when I reached it, dire anticipation gave way to fear. That door was going to open, and though I knew it would be bad form to grab the knob and hold it shut, the thought crossed my mind. Molly's mother, furiously angry and distraught, opened the door with body language that showed I was invited in, but I wasn't welcome. Charlie Kirkwood, father of sophomore guard Kimmy Kirkwood, was in the living room. Apparently, he would be the mediator.

I sat on their couch and let Jen take the lead. I could hear Molly sobbing in another room and I wondered how long the pleasantries would last before we got to the heart of the moment. Thankfully, small-talk was not invited, and Jen commenced her interrogation before I sunk into their living room couch. Jen told me how Molly had to force one-word sentences through her tears, and that she'd never seen her oldest daughter so upset. Jen couldn't understand why I'd blindsided her daughter. She was a mother moose protecting her calf from a surprise attack by a grizzly bear.

"Molly's name is on the readerboard for the varsity and you moved a freshman ahead of her," Jen said sitting across from me, arms crossed. "Why didn't you warn her?" Before I could get two words out, mediator Charlie jumped in. "I'm pretty sure that Bill's view was, 'If we don't go to state, I don't have to hurt your daughter,'" he said. "Bill didn't say anything until he knew we were going to state." Still, Jen insisted that I should have done something earlier to better prepare Molly and her family.

Jen argued that Allison and Colleen weren't likely to even play in the state tournament games. "Why couldn't it be my daughter who gets to suit up and sit on the bench?" she asked, over the agonizing sound of Molly's sobbing. "There are four games in a row," I told her. "You never know what may happen. I made a decision that I thought was best for the team, and I hurt your daughter's feelings and I feel like hell about it." I told her that I didn't expect Allison Reiman and Colleen Bresee to play at state, but it was possible. I was making a statistical choice to win the games, and though I'm not about winning or losing, I have an ethical duty to the team to put the best players on the court. But whether we win state or lose state doesn't matter. Molly matters. And I'd just broken her heart.

After about an hour, we agreed that Molly should join the conversation in the living room, and when she did, she was a mess. I explained to her that the chosen girls are better basketball players than her, but they're not better people, and that I could have made a mistake. Coaching involves a lot of guesswork. Molly wasn't a bad player, I told them. I went on to explain that Roosevelt is an elite program. KingCo 4A is one of Washington State's toughest leagues. Some rival coaches think it's *the* toughest. Roosevelt had more than 1,600 students during each of Molly's years as a varsity athlete. With the amount of sheer talent that shows up at our tryouts, we could send a Roosevelt freshman team to beat some Seattle high schools. If Molly didn't play with such talented teammates, she'd be a standout. As I told Molly this, she made the selfless comments of a true martyr. I felt as if I'd just told Mother Teresa that she needed to work a little harder.

I can't remember Molly's exact words. Many of those moments are too painful for me to recall. My basic philosophy is not to worry about what you can't control, and you can't control the past. But I always rethink my choices because that's how the life lessons surface. And when it came to cutting Molly from the state championship-team, I'm not certain I made the right choice.

In our first game at state, all 12 girls played and we crushed Gig Harbor 52–29. This not only gave the two freshmen the reward of playing at state, it also gave the team's main rotation much-needed rest before the quarterfinals. Eleven girls contributed to our 59–50 win against Lewis and Clark in the quarterfinals, and all 12 played when we edged Snohomish 58–54, advancing to the state championship game for the first time in Roosevelt's history. Going into the championship game, our starters were far more rested than those of our opponent.

Typically, the state championship leads to a face-off between two teams that have never played each other. Instead, in the 2004 state championship we played Garfield—the first time in state history that teams from the same league played for the state's highest honor. I hadn't forgotten our league championship loss to Garfield, or the 21-point pounding they'd delivered during that regular season game. But I also hadn't forgotten my overall belief that experiencing the moment was more important than winning, so I decided to play all 12 girls in the championship game, even if it cost us the game.

Allison and Colleen played. Molly watched from the bench in her Roosevelt basketball T-shirt. Even worse, Molly's parents watched from the stands. I wondered if they recalled me sitting in their living room when I suggested, "It doesn't matter—we're probably not going to play everyone." As it turned out, it mattered more than ever.

Although Molly didn't play, she was integral to the outcome. She was more vocal than I was on the bench, screaming at teammates to box out and drop-into help defense. The game was war-like, but despite the intensity, Molly found a way to ensure that her teammates had fun. When we gave up a 7-point halftime lead and trailed 43–40 late in the third quarter, Molly still exuded confidence. I don't know what she said, but I know she cut the tension by making clusters of girls laugh. Honestly, it doesn't really matter what she said, but whatever it was, it worked like a charm. Like a soldier doing her duty, Molly had accepted her role, and though she didn't show up on the stat sheet, she undoubtedly contributed to our 55–52 state championship victory.

Many teenagers are myopic, unable to see beyond what affects them at the personal level. But Molly's focus was the greater good of her friends, which was obvious to us all by the way she engaged her teammates. She listened, understood, gave feedback, and came to practice even after the most humiliating setbacks. There were practices where she couldn't completely hide her emotional pain, and her face sometimes showed a smile with subtle tears. But she inspired her teammates regardless of how up or down her emotions were. Her goal wasn't to be inspiring. Nobody chooses to be the Rudy. But by providing the example, she inspired people. She epitomized the belief that you can't have a championship team without sacrifice.

Because making a basket or beating the opponent isn't that important to Molly, she didn't work on embarrassing opponents. Molly wanted to be a teammate, and she also wanted to be a true friend. Shellacking an opponent was not on her menu. Some girls can't handle losing and are driven to succeed. As a Roughrider, Molly didn't want to lose, but there was more to her than that. She saw a broader spectrum than winning and losing. Unfortunately, the manic-driven are more often than not the winning athletes who get playing time and play on successful teams.

As a junior, Molly's game improved, but several younger girls had clearly overtaken her. After the second day of tryouts, I pulled Molly aside and had another brutal conversation with her. I tried to be as delicate as possible as I explained that she wouldn't play in close games. Her skill level wasn't as good as the ten girls ahead of her, a pack that included her freshman sister. It was a miserable conversation that left Molly in tears. I didn't know if she could handle her role. I didn't want a hurricane like I created during Molly's sophomore year, but I had to be honest with her. It wouldn't have surprised me if she'd decided to quit. I didn't want her to, but it might have been the only way for her to leave the team with her ego intact. After our conversation, she left the room with her head hanging. I didn't know what would happen next. While trying to avoid the storm, it was possible that I'd invited a Category 5 hurricane into our locker room.

The next day before practice, Molly pulled me aside and told me that I'd really hurt her feelings during our conversation. I apologized and explained that had never been my intention. I only wanted to be honest with her, and give her a chance to understand her role. I didn't want her to be blindsided if she didn't get much playing time as the season progressed, I explained. Telling Molly all of this was difficult and awkward, but it later produced that silver lining that every well-meaning coach hopes for. Molly wasn't able to confront me as a sophomore, but as a junior she expressed her honest feelings directly to me, without putting up a barrier. That's a skill that some people never learn in a lifetime. And for me, that was a big-time payout. Even the president of the drama club knows a high school coach's pay is miniscule. If a coach is in it for the money, that coach should trade his or her playbook for a lifetime subscription to the *Wall Street Journal*. Participating in progress like Molly's is worth more than the all-time Publishers Clearinghouse payout.

The team did not do well during Molly's junior season. We opened with four wins, then suffered a five-game losing streak, highlighted by three blowouts in a holiday tournament that we hosted. We never beat Garfield or Redmond and lost five of our last six games. Molly, who scored only 11 points in 17 games, had no plans to dominate the league as a basketball player. But she liked her teammates, which is what kept her coming back. She had effort in practice, but she never let it all hang out. I don't think she gave her all partly due to a fear of failure and partly due to her role on the team. It isn't easy going all out in practice after your coach tells you he's limiting your playing time. It doesn't ease the tension to know that with a different coach, she wouldn't have played at all.

I'd considered cutting Molly. I didn't because without her, the team would have collapsed. Alex Capeloto and Laura Mohler—teammates the same age as Molly who played in the state championship game—

said that if Molly had quit, they would have gone with her. And I knew there were more Roughriders who felt the same way.

By the time she was a senior, Molly knew her stuff, she just couldn't perform as well as her teammates. She could recite the intricacies of our complex system in five languages. She was a seasoned veteran who didn't hesitate to send freshmen into walls during practices. But in games, she was a different player. When Molly had the ball, she froze. She was too worried about making mistakes and when a player worries about making mistakes, rarely are her stats impressive.

Molly started on the Senior Night game, and at a pre-season game at Key Arena in which I started all seniors. She also started in a playoff game because teammate Maggie Torrance asked me to start all seniors out of superstition. Maggie said it was because we beat that playoff opponent on Senior Night. I suspect part of it was to make sure Molly would start. During Molly's senior year, I started her in the second game we played at the state tournament as a minor payback for the hurt I'd caused her two years earlier. Besides those exceptions, Molly usually played only when Roosevelt was expected to win with ease.

We were expected to win a regular season game against Juanita High, a team that had never come close to beating us and that had finished 1–19 in the 2005–06 season. In games against weaker opponents, I play up-and-coming varsity and JV players almost as much as the main rotation. Two days before the Juanita game, Molly and her four senior teammates asked me to meet with them in the equipment room—the same room where I'd had the miserable task of informing Molly she wouldn't get many minutes.

The girls told me that they wanted Kassy Griswold and Cameron Miller to get significant playing time against Juanita. Kassy and Cameron were juniors who knew they wouldn't make the varsity as seniors because there were simply too many players ranked ahead of them. "I don't really get that many minutes, but I want to give all my minutes to Kassy and Cameron," Molly said, knowing that these two girls had no other chances to play for the Roosevelt varsity. I hung around the equipment room after the meeting, not knowing whether to laugh or cry at what Molly told me. Here was a girl who rarely got playing time, and when she knew she would be in for most the game, volunteered to ride the bench to benefit her teammates. It was the first time in my eight-year career that senior varsity players had volunteered to give up their precious playing minutes to benefit their JV teammates.

When Molly recalls her experience as a Roughrider, what I hope she realizes is that her minutes were secondary to her spirit, and it was her spirit that fueled our state championship drive. If Molly knew how essential she was to her teammates' success back then, she never bragged about it. She didn't take credit at all. "It's them," she told the *Seattle Post-Intelligencer* in a feature story about her. "They're the ones scoring." Each one of the girls deserves a feature story, she said. She talked of teammate Alex Capeloto who could hit a shot from anywhere and teammate Laura Mohler who treated practice like the fourth quarter of a playoff game. When the reporter asked about her pep talk to junior Mackenzie Argens after she missed three consecutive shots in a 69–66 overtime loss to Newport, Molly talked instead about Mackenzie's confidence and the coordination she's gained since her freshman year.

Did Molly make the right choice to stay on the team, through her humiliation and five gallons of tears? Teenagers' brains are undergoing constant change. In this respect, teenagers can't fully understand the implications of their actions, or grasp the lessons they're learning while they're in the moment. The right time to ask Molly if she made the right choice should be when she's 30, not when she's in high school.

Each spring, parents and students gather in the Roosevelt gym for a winter sport banquet. Each team announces a single team award in front of the 400-plus crowd, before they head off to separate rooms to distribute their letter awards. The girls basketball team doesn't select a Most Valuable Player award—this singular type of recognition doesn't build a cohesive team. Instead, Roosevelt celebrates and awards the best defender, the most improved, and the most inspirational athletes. On other teams, it might be the coach who decides which players deserve any awards. I leave the decisions up to the team. The Inner Circle has taught me that 12 young minds know far more than my old one. At the end of Molly's junior season, I got to deliver one of my favorite speeches.

"For the first time ever, we have a unanimous winner for an award," I told the crowd, who started chanting Molly's name seconds after I finished the sentence. Anybody living within 50 miles of Roosevelt knew who was going to walk on stage to accept the award for Most Inspirational Player. I gave a short speech, and Molly accepted the honor. When she sat down, I returned to the microphone and admitted that I lied. "It wasn't really unanimous," I told the audience. "Molly voted for somebody else."

When all is said and done, it's not the stats that matter, nor the final scores. It's the heart and spirit of a player that matter. And I hope Molly knows that we could never have won that championship title without her sacrifice.

CHAPTER SEVEN

Maggie Torrance

Maggie Torrance (Photograph by Casey McNerthney)

Know the Difference Between Work and Play

Everybody has heard the phrase "Work hard, play hard." But I tell my teams "Work hard, play hard. Don't get the two confused and move quickly from one to the other." The difference is subtle, but I believe it's crucial for success.

I think the biggest mistake people make is they waste time and happiness by mixing work and play. Teenagers are especially guilty of this bungle. Impatience causes all of us to want to find an immediate conclusion instead of inching our way towards perfection. This often leads us to wish we were playing when we're working, and on the flipside, worrying about work when we're playing. In this way, we fail to get the most out of or enjoy either of them. If a player came to practice with an iPod, she would be able to listen to music while working on her game. The music would add to her enjoyment of playing, but it would distract her mightily from skill and team improvement, thereby damaging all her work efforts. However, the player can make the best of both worlds by listening to her iPod during water breaks, and taking it off and leaving it on the sidelines while on the court practicing.

Basketball practice is the perfect place to pound home this message. When we run drills, Roosevelt players must give an all-out aggression or they'll hear from me, and in a manner they'd rather avoid. No drills are longer than eight minutes, and I schedule frequent water breaks so the girls can relax with the same intensity. By the time they're upperclassmen, the girls have figured out how to laugh during drills and still bring their game on as hard as they can.

In my eight years as head coach, I've never had a player who better exemplified the work-hard-play-hard mentality than Maggie Torrance. But when she arrived in the gym as an eighth-grader about to enter Roosevelt, she really didn't have a clue about managing work and play in a way that would allow her to experience the best of both worlds.

Before her arrival at Roosevelt, I was warned about Maggie. More than a dozen parents and teachers told me she was an amazing soul, but to watch out for her. "In what way?" I asked. It was said she had a temper that made John McEnroe look like a puppy dog. I asked for examples, but all I got were obtuse general warnings. I cross-examined, but each warning in return was a weak, sweeping statement. It was frustrating, but nevertheless, I'd been warned.

From the first moment she entered the Roosevelt gym in 2002, I could tell that Maggie's personality was distinct. Each summer, I invite incoming freshmen to the gym for summer practices. Most eighth-graders are timid and intimidated by coaches and the varsity players who also attend. Maggie came in, figured out I was the head coach, strode up to me, and stuck out her hand. She looked in my eyes as she introduced herself, showing from that first moment that she was not a typical teenager.

Maggie wasn't a good dribbler. She wasn't exceptionally quick. There was nothing special about her shot. But it soon became clear that Maggie had something about her that nobody else had: a starter engine that allowed her to draw a knife and slit an opponent's throat to win a game. She'd knock opponents down without thinking twice about it. When seniors criticized her, which was common for under-classmen, she blew them off. She didn't fire back; instead she proceeded on as if nothing had occurred. At 14, she had the kind of self-confidence some people never develop in a lifetime. I thought, "My God, this girl might learn to be a varsity basketball player."

She developed her basic basketball skills from her dad, Bill Torrance, a former Roughrider who stressed that defense wins games. If she had exceptional defense, Bill told his daughter, her offense would come. From the first day Maggie played in elementary school, achieving seven steals and eight assists meant much more to her than a double digit scoring performance. She was so aggressive on defense that her middle school teachers banned her from playing recess basketball because they feared her play as too big a liability. Each time a Roosevelt classmate knocked Maggie for not scoring as many points as other girls, she hit back with a standard response: "Come watch me play. You'll see what I do for my team."

During Maggie's first week of Roughrider practices, her teammates wore bruises from her accidental elbows and her insane dives into their legs for loose balls. She was often criticized for being too hard on the court, but Maggie, who was the youngest in a family of three, never relented. When teammates told her to slow down, and that she didn't need to get so rough in practice, she didn't seem to understand their reasoning and never acted as though she cared to. Maggie wanted to win at all times and at all costs, whether she was playing in the state championship or a summer practice pick-up game. "When I see a girl coming at me who wants to block me with an illegal moving screen," Maggie explained with a rich grin, "I plan to knock her on her ass. She's going to get the foul, and she's going to pay for it."

What Maggie was thinking, people heard without a filter. When a teammate biffed a practice play, some girls offered careful, constructive criticism. They'd say something like "Hey, if you dribble into the corner, it'll probably result in a turnover. If you try to avoid that, things might work out better." Maggie's analysis would come out as, "You're a (bleeping) moron. Stay out of the (bleeping) corner." One could say Maggie has a way with words.

Some of Maggie's teammates spent every day worrying about what would happen in the upcoming basketball season, but didn't go all out to improve their basketball skills during practice. But that wasn't Maggie's style. When she was playing basketball, she was there to win at that moment, and she gave exhausting energy until the final whistle. But when she left the court, Maggie had her own life.

I told her how good she'd be if she practiced during the off-season, like her teammates. She thought about it, but said she wanted a full life, not just a basketball life. When it wasn't basketball season, Maggie was a typical teenager hanging out with friends. During summers, she spent time at her family's cabin north of Seattle. Basketball season was for basketball, Maggie said, and her off-time was for her to play hard.

After tryouts, Maggie was selected for the junior varsity (impressive for a freshman), but Maggie wanted more and not making varsity was the end of her world. When I told her that she'd made the JV team, she surprised me with a single look that revealed both sadness and anger. Maggie had immense self-confidence and she knew she was better than the other freshmen who were ranked above her after tryouts. But at this point in her game, Maggie didn't understand that her eighth-grade basketball skills were woefully inadequate for high school ball. And as a ninth-grader, it was hard for Maggie to comprehend the amount of talent within Roosevelt's elite program. With her experience, it was hard for her to realize that her game still had a long way to go until she was ready for the varsity.

The starter engine that powered Maggie's throat-slitting aggression soon became evident. She'd knock opponents down in nearly every game. Although a couple of freshmen had more offensive skills, no one had Maggie's fire and desire to win. Feeling that the varsity would benefit from an injection of such ferocity, we moved her up. This annoyed other freshman players who'd long ago tired of Maggie's in-your-face attitude. At Roosevelt, we try to teach our teams to support and enjoy their teammates' success. Unfortunately for Maggie, when we moved her up to varsity, not all of her teammates could overcome their envy.

When Maggie was a freshman, our current seniors hadn't quite learned how to be effective leaders. Some seniors were afraid that underclassmen would steal playing time that they thought they deserved more than underlings. This tension culminated into the seniors confronting the underclassmen about their own insecurities, causing mistrust and bickering among teammates. During Maggie's freshman season, she experienced team leaders who showed that they cared more about their own achievements than those of the team as a whole.

I've learned that seniors preside over any team, and though they can make incorrect leadership decisions, it's their first chance to be boss of the block. Seniority provides upperclassmen with their first chance to lead, and the system works because of high school pecking order. I sometimes view all my young players as fledgling angels with brand new wings. They fly off carrying the best intentions, and crash every so often because they're neophytes who haven't yet learned how to correctly flap their wings. By the time they're seniors they crash much less often; nevertheless, they still crash.

Maggie realized that some older players were better than her as a freshman, and since she wanted to win at all costs, she didn't mind sitting on the bench if it helped the team. As she got older, Maggie demanded more playing time—not because she was selfish, but because she believed the team would be strongest with her on the court.

As a coach, I can tell by the way teammates compete in drills and laugh in practice whether or not the team will have a winning record. This particular season, the seniors lacked the dedication required to make Roosevelt a state-caliber team. As an example, open gyms—which are held independent of coaches—usually last about 90 minutes. Following this, the girls often retreat to the weight room for an additional half-hour workout. For this particular season, open gyms rarely lasted an hour, and only a few of the players went to the weight room afterward. The girls also lacked the ultimate focus of championship basketball players. I wanted this team to enjoy a season of memorable practices. So, in early October that year, I held a team meeting and explained that if their overall attitude and work ethic didn't change for the better, the Roughriders would be a 13–7 team.

Later, a senior told me that she agreed with everything I'd said, which gave me hope that the team would right their listing ship. I was certain that if they understood the importance of working hard on the court and playing hard when off the court, the team would be more successful. But sadly, my speech didn't do the trick—none of the seniors stepped up to change the situation after the team meeting.

Not surprisingly, we were flat when the season started and opened with two losses. When our record was 4–4, I called another team meeting. "We have our regular players who do a good job, and then we've got these other players who rarely get in the game," I told the girls. "We've got to find a way to mix it up and change things. So, we're going to have a new squad called the Assassin Squad. The Assassins' job is to go in for 90 seconds, double-team the ball at all times, and wear the other team down while the more experienced players take a rest."

Maggie's eyes lit up immediately as I explained the Assassin Squad because she knew this would be *her* squad. "When are the Assassin tryouts?" Maggie asked, barely able to sit still. "Tomorrow," I announced. Maggie locked her eyes on me like a hungry wolf: "*I'm so there!*" There wasn't a doubt in my mind that Maggie's DNA and life experience made her perfect for this role. In a shock to no one, Maggie led the Assassins.

By the end of her freshman year, Maggie had proven to be tenacious, always there for the team, full of humor, and unwilling to take grief from anyone. In practices, whenever Maggie was criticized for her maniacal play, she would either ignore the person or tell them off. Frankly, I felt Maggie had a marvelous freshman campaign, though I worried at how she struggled with separating work from play, and vice versa. For her age, Maggie was fairly focused. She knew how to work hard and how to play hard, but she didn't move quickly between them. And, she clearly would get both work and play confused. Maggie was so driven that she often failed to see the humor in the inevitable mistakes that are part of the human condition. Also, sometimes getting Maggie to the gym could be difficult, but once she was there, she was a tireless worker.

During her sophomore year, following that 15–9 season, Maggie started to become the player I had been warned about. Late in our opening season game against Issaquah, we trailed in a close game and were forced to foul so we could get possessions and snatch a victory. Fouling our opponents would give them a free throw. If Issaquah missed and Roosevelt rebounded the ball, we'd get a much-needed possession. It's a pretty standard coaching strategy.

I yelled from the sideline that we needed to foul the girl, so Maggie ran to one of the guards and threw a forearm towards the girl's cheekbone. The Issaquah girl had barely hit the ground when the referee whistled Maggie for a flagrant foul and ejected her from the game. Sometimes, she took her work-hard mentality too far. To be called for the much-needed foul, Maggie merely had to gently swipe at the ball. Maggie's raw hatred of losing, though, caused her to miss the point that basketball is just a game. Maggie's extreme foul gave Issaquah *two* free throws and, even worse, they retained possession of the ball after the free throws. I explained after the 49–38 loss that the reason we foul in a situation like that is to get possession, and with a flagrant foul we don't get possession. "Well, you say that every foul should be a hard foul," Maggie retorted. As usual, her gifted brain allowed her to find the perfect lawyer response, even if it wasn't accurate.

When someone is 17, they believe they're right. When they're 17 and smart, they believe they're always right. During her teen years, Maggie traveled the road of life believing she had it all figured out. She would draw her own conclusions and then would reason backwards to prove each conclusion. Thanks to her agile brain, she became quite good at it. Still, she had plenty more to learn as a sophomore.

During a game against Franklin, Maggie was assigned to guard their senior star, who immediately realized she could take Maggie out of her game by talking trash. Through most of the second half, the girl played Maggie like a violin, pushing her to the brink with a barrage of ugly comments. Maggie was shorter and not nearly as built as the Franklin girl, but that didn't stop her from getting her hands around the trash-talking opponent's neck. As Maggie was ejected, I noticed the smile on the Franklin player's face. That victory in the bigger game of life was hers.

After our team meeting, I told Maggie she'd been played by the Franklin senior and that it was an important lesson for her to experience. "In the future, you want to be the girl who gets in other people's heads instead of letting them get to you," I said.

One of Maggie's most important life-lesson moments occurred near the end of her sophomore year, when she started in the league championship against Garfield. Roosevelt was ahead 38–30 at the end of three quarters, and needed only a few buckets to pull away with the victory. Instead, we turned the ball over on our first four possessions of the fourth quarter, and fired air balls on the fifth and sixth possessions. Late that same quarter, Garfield was at the free-throw line. We needed a rebound, and that meant we needed Mackenzie Argens—a 6-foot-2 freshman and the team's tallest player. I called Maggie out and subbed in Mackenzie so she could snag that important rebound. But 5-foot-6 Maggie didn't understand my reasoning.

She was a sobbing mess when she took her seat on the bench. I was caught completely off-guard. The same girl that could run roughshod over an opponent was sobbing uncontrollably, and I had no idea how to console her. She wanted to win more than she wanted air at that point, and from her perspective, I was a backstabber. The game went into overtime and we needed Maggie's toughness for those pulsating four minutes. Her desire to win made her regain her composure, but Garfield went on a 5–0 run at the end of overtime and won by four.

After the game, I explained probabilities to Maggie—that by substituting a taller girl for her at that crucial time, I was increasing our chances of winning. I told her she must keep her wits about her during future games because we needed her amazing skills. I hoped Maggie listened, but she was so angry I didn't know what was getting through.

We earned the league's second state berth with a win against Redmond the following night, and eight days and three state victories later, we faced Garfield for the third time—this time for the 4A state championship.

This year the new theme for the girls to latch onto was Pack of Wolves. All season, I told the girls how wolves are the only animal gutsy enough to return a man's stare, and showed them pictures of snarling, staring wolves. The girls thought this was a cheesy tactic, but even so, they admitted it got their blood flowing before games. "I have one question for you," I asked in the locker room before we faced the Bulldogs. "Are you dogs or are you wolves?" Several girls screamed out, "We're wolves!" Maggie tilted up her head and howled. Once again, Maggie was in the moment.

Garfield opened the game with a 9–0 explosion. We couldn't score in the first three minutes and were dying for a basket when Maggie launched a rainbow from the right corner. That 3-pointer ignited us, and we ended the quarter tied at 11. We walloped Garfield in the second quarter and the Roughriders rode a 7-point lead into the locker room.

When I entered the halftime locker room, Maggie and our star player Darnellia Russell sat side-by-side jabbering about basketball strategy. Maggie had a close relationship with Darnellia, partially because Darnellia was the only girl who could tell her to "shut up" and have it register, although she never said it directly. Darnellia had the ability to merely *glance* at a teammate to deliver a three-paragraph speech. Maggie listened to her because Darnellia wanted to win every bit as much as Maggie did, if not more. They were kindred spirits.

Garfield overtook us in the third quarter, and it felt like there were a zillion lead changes in the emotion-filled fourth quarter. We crawled ahead 54–52 with 5.6 seconds remaining when Garfield's

LaCale Pringle was sent to the free-throw line. She missed her first free throw and the Bulldogs called time-out. We knew LaCale would intentionally miss the shot so the Bulldogs could get the rebound and tie the game up with a field goal. The state championship was riding on that rebound.

We desperately needed to get that rebound and to have a chance against the much taller Bulldogs, and that meant putting Mackenzie on the court. I screamed this to the players in what was the game's most chaotic huddle ever, and just as I was about to call one of the players out so Mackenzie could go in, Maggie ran around from the back of the huddle to get my attention. "She can go in for me," she said. "I'm short." At that spectacular instant, winning the game had turned into icing on the cake in Maggie's head. Eight days prior she'd been a sobbing mess when the same substitution had been called; but now she had learned to sacrifice herself for the team.

As suspected, LaCale missed the shot on purpose and we got the ball back. And in the tensest seconds of my life, Roosevelt beat Garfield 55–52 for the school's first state title.

Maggie had finally seen the importance of making personal sacrifices for the greater good of the team, but her inability to control her temper and physical aggression was holding her back. During the summer league games before her junior year, Maggie seemed to receive more technical fouls than points. She swore at other players, swore at referees, and swore at me. If she felt like checking a girl into the bleachers, she did. In some instances, my assistant coach, Wayne Seward, had to leave the game to sit with her in the concourse of the arena because she'd been ejected. When her outbursts were out of control as an underclassman, Maggie blamed her anger on referees or the coaching staff—anybody but herself. But that summer, Maggie became enlightened. "Why can't I control myself?" She blurted to Wayne through a waterfall of tears. "What's going wrong?

Why do I do this?" It was a breakthrough moment: she had finally realized that she was responsible for her unacceptable behavior, and it was causing her problems. From that moment on, a new Maggie emerged. She began to take control of her emotions, to restrain her aggression, and to cut back on her ill tempers.

As players mature, I noticed that they realize their mistakes more frequently. They also realize that I don't judge them by their mistakes, but by how they correct them. But not all adults share my view. Take former Redmond coach Pat Bangasser.

If Roosevelt has ever liked players from Redmond, it was long before I started coaching. Some Redmond players have said we have no class, and our players counter that Redmond players are entitled snobs. I believe such teenage bickering always occurs in any good rivalry, but it should end with coaches. It was no secret among KingCo 4A league players and coaches that if someone could really get into Maggie's head, she'd become so enraged that her game would sink into the toilet. Since she was so tough, and because her blowups were famous as the league's most dramatic, she was an opponent teams loved to hate.

During a regular-season game against Redmond, the Mustangs' coach, Pat Bangasser, taunted Maggie from the sidelines. He screamed to the referee that she was a dangerous player who was out of control. She was a threat to injure someone, he yelled, and must be taken out of the game. The younger Maggie would have erupted, and screamed back at him, or maybe even tried to choke him like she did that Franklin girl. But she'd matured—she kept her cool and recognized how ridiculous Pat's taunting was. "I'm the stupid teenager," she told me on the sidelines. "What the (bleep) is his problem?"

After that Redmond game, Pat approached me still furious about Maggie's angry play, which he complained was reckless. He ranted about her foul mouth that lacked a censor. He hated how she knocked girls down when they tried to set illegal screens on her. "What are you going to do about Maggie Torrance?" he asked. I told him that I thought Maggie was a work in progress. I could have given up on her when she was a sophomore, but you can't force life lessons. You have to develop them through experiences and Maggie was still developing. Pat wasn't able to see it that way.

But during the final seconds of the biggest game of Maggie's life, Pat hadn't seen the girl he wanted off the court as she offered herself up, allowing me to sub in long-legs Mackenzie. He didn't see the restraint she'd developed over the past two seasons. He didn't ever get to see the Maggie I knew, so therefore, he didn't know who she was now, and how far she'd come. Maybe when you have a rivalry as big and intense as Redmond's rivalry with Roosevelt, it's difficult to see an opposing player's progress. Although I think it's difficult to do, as a coach I think it's important to care about the personal growth of all young players, even those on opposing teams. Our focus shouldn't be on trouncing our rivals into a pulp. Instead, we need to keep the bigger picture in mind: that it's important for all teens to develop skills that will take them far on and off the court, and that we shouldn't jump to conclusions about players we don't work with on a daily basis.

During Maggie's junior year, we had no seniors, and seniors are crucial to any team. Not only did all of our seniors graduate, we also lost Darnellia Russell, Roosevelt's most compelling leader. Without leaders, there was no way that we'd make a return trip to state. No miracle happened that season, and we were bounced out of the playoffs early.

This situation caused new problems for Maggie, who wanted to continue at a state-championship pace—she continued fighting for every loose ball and taking out any teammates that got in her way. Maggie was the alpha female, but instead of following her lead, the four other juniors backed away from her because they took her verbal bashings as personal insults, instead of uncensored encouragement intended to make them better players. These girls weren't about to follow a leader who used a sledgehammer to get her point across.

Maggie refused to lose even during the most mundane practice drills, and she became increasingly hostile. Many of her junior teammates were there to have fun and though they also wanted to win, they didn't become furious over a loss. We experienced a five-game losing streak during the first half of our season, and before the first loss the schism between Maggie and the four other juniors had grown to the point that practices became head-down sullen. During water breaks, Maggie sat alone at one corner of the gym. The other girls gossiped and talked in groups at another corner.

I met with Maggie several times to try and repair what was tearing the team's fabric to shreds. Maggie didn't understand why her teammates didn't play with the same all-out aggression as she did. Maggie didn't want to argue; she wanted to win and she couldn't believe that her teammates wouldn't try to at all costs. Maggie's teammates told me they couldn't get past her fire-breathing criticisms that I understood were meant to motivate them.

We held several Inner Circle meetings to try to resolve this divide. The purpose of the Inner Circle is to teach the girls to solve their own problems and to keep parents and coaches from meddling in the decision-making process. Nevertheless, in this situation some juniors shared the problem with their parents. Several of those parents told me that Maggie deserved this cold-shoulder treatment because they'd witnessed her rough behavior for years and they wanted no more of it. I explained that no one deserved to be detested in that manner, but Maggie's teammates and some parents didn't understand, and didn't agree.

When Maggie realized this divide was tearing our team apart, she called the team together in the locker room before practice. Reading from a two-page handwritten letter, she apologized for her out-of-control behavior. She didn't want to act that way, she said, and she didn't want her teammates to dislike her. She also expressed that some of her teammates' actions made her feel miserable. Maggie couldn't get through the first page before she broke into tears.

Before Maggie came along, I'd never witnessed a player be so mistreated by her teammates. And I'd also never seen a player make herself as vulnerable as Maggie did in that meeting as she expressed her honest, root emotions to teammates who lacked her same courage. But unfortunately, Maggie's words hit some players' foreheads and just dropped to the ground without penetrating. When Maggie's speech was over, teammates said they understood, but their actions said otherwise. Maggie didn't get heartfelt hugs and acknowledgement for her apologies, or her courage for being so open, or trying to right a bad situation. Maggie's teammates didn't give her the clean slate she'd hoped for, and deserved.

A few days later, Maggie asked me why her teammates hadn't opened up and shared their feelings, or at least tried to understand where she was coming from. "They made a mistake," I told her. "Help them fix it by showing that you can move past it." Maggie did just that, demonstrating a new upbeat and jovial mood at practices. If she judged her teammates over their bullheadedness, she didn't show it. I became increasingly impressed watching this 17-year-old furiously work her tail off in practice, then transition into a carefree teenager who joined her teammates at water breaks. It showed that Maggie knew how to work hard, how to play hard, and had learned the difference between the two.

In her underclassman days, Maggie often lamented that she should be working on her game when she was off the court. Maggie always went hard in practice. When she wasn't in practice, she played hard at life. By her senior year, she'd embraced the idea of moving from work to play as rapidly as possible. Though coaches and teammates tried to get her to be a year-round basketball player, Maggie didn't let basketball get in the way of play. She didn't lift weights. She didn't run sprints to condition herself in the summer. Her time off the court was spent on her family's boat, or hanging out with her boyfriend. It didn't matter what people told her as a senior—she designated her time to maximize her enjoyment.

During Maggie's senior year, Roosevelt had a hearing- and speech-impaired girl on the JVC team. Despite her disabilities, the girl was as free-spirited as any player I've ever seen, laughing at the coaches' jokes and running through drills with that all-fun mentality that comes with many high school sports teams. But she couldn't really connect with her teammates because she had difficulty communicating.

Late in the season, I found out that Maggie and the hearing-impaired player had been writing notes to each other almost daily. I don't know when it started. None of the adults knew about the notes, and I only learned about them because one was left sitting out at practice. I'd bet that Maggie waited for just the right time to exchange notes with the girl, when no one else would see. She wasn't being her friend because she wanted credit. Maggie was her friend because she truly cared about this teammate.

Maggie said she felt like hell when her unusual aggression kept teammates from wanting to be around her. When she watched her deaf teammate during practice, Maggie experienced a new epiphany. She realized how lonely it must have been for the girl who was just like everyone else, but who was shut out in certain ways by her teammates because they felt like they couldn't communicate with her, and they didn't try to solve that problem. Maggie didn't want this teammate to be an outcast. She knew what that felt like. "If you ever want to talk," she wrote in the first note, "you can talk to me."

After the basketball season, I was told that Maggie's new friend was being transferred to a school designed specifically for hearing-impaired students. I hadn't told the team, but somehow Maggie had learned of the news. I was walking through the halls late in the school day when Maggie ran up to me. "There's no reason to transfer her to a special school," Maggie said. "She needs to be in the mainstream. She's doing well at Roosevelt." I explained that the decision had already been made by the girl's parents, and there was nothing I could do. Maggie's vocabulary and way of expressing frustration had evolved, and this time she expressed herself in a way that showed how much she truly cared about her teammate. Knee-jerk critics said Maggie was reckless, and only cared about herself. It's a pity that their jealousy didn't allow them to know the real Maggie Torrance, who remained friends with the deaf girl long after she left Roosevelt.

During summer games before her senior year, I was able to count Maggie's technical fouls on one hand. "When you see me starting to blow up, say something to me," she begged teammates in an early season meeting. During huddles, Maggie would say things like, "I'm probably wrong, but if you come out and help on the weak side then I can defend the guard." She wasn't wrong for a second and she knew it, but Maggie had learned how to be a teacher. She was no longer all about herself. She wanted her younger teammates to listen because she knew what would be best for her team, and in order to do that, she'd changed her ways. At a certain level, I don't think she cared what her teammates were thinking. Maggie just cared that we won games, and she knew that when she lost her teammates' respect, we lost games.

Late in her senior season, we had a tense matchup against Garfield. We played even for most of the game, but by the fourth quarter Garfield's size had taken its toll and we were down by 6. With five minutes remaining and Roosevelt still behind, I took Maggie out. She thought I was giving up on the game by inserting less experienced players. My assistant, Wayne Seward, who'd been monitoring Maggie over the years to see when she might reach her breaking point, saw in her face that a catastrophe was eminent and warned me to cool her down. I only said, "Get some water." All the players decoded that missive: Maggie will be going back in. She sat for 90 seconds and said, "Bill, I'm ready." I grinned at her. "It's about time," I joked.

Many fans thought the game was over when Garfield went up 57–45 with just over three minutes remaining. "You guys are good enough to beat them," I said during a time-out. "Just go out there, let it all hang out, and have fun. Show them how good you are." I relied on Maggie's spirit to ignite the team.

During the second half, Garfield's LaCale Pringle hit her first six shots—including four of four from 3-point range—on her way to a game-high of 21 points. Maggie, who always wanted to guard the opponent's best player, insisted on guarding LaCale. In the three and a half minutes that Maggie glued herself to LaCale, the Garfield player wasn't able to score. When I called for someone on the team to intentionally foul, Maggie told her teammates that it couldn't be her. She had four fouls already and didn't want to foul out by getting more. The old Maggie wouldn't have cared, but this Maggie was in control of her emotions.

With 48 seconds on the clock, we fouled LaCale. This time, she missed her first and air-balled the second. We pulled within 5 during the final minute and with 40 seconds left, senior Alex Capeloto hit a 3-pointer from the right corner to put us within 2. At this point, Garfield should have run some clock off, but instead they launched an errant shot that was rebounded by junior Mackenzie Argens. She passed to Maggie, who sent back a pass on a play that ended with Mackenzie's left-hand layin. With ten seconds to go, the game was tied at 57.

LaCale brought the ball up court, hounded by Maggie. When she passed the ball, Maggie dove, sacrificing her body to keep Garfield from scoring. She got the tips of her right hand on the ball, allowing Mackenzie to grab the wounded-duck pass and drive the length of the court for another left-handed layin with 3.6 seconds remaining. Garfield called time-out, and I had to find a way to keep them from getting off a reasonable shot. I wanted Garfield to inbound the ball by their baseline, forcing them to huck the ball the length of the court and making a reasonable shot nearly impossible. To create this scenario, I told the team to play a 1-2-2 soft full-court zone.

"Like hell we're going to do that!" Maggie shrieked in the huddle. "Yes, we're going to run a 1-2-2 zone and I'm going to show you why," I said. I drew the play on the white coaching board during the timeout. She looked at it and nodded. "Oh, yeah, that's perfect," she said. Garfield had to launch a prayer. We won 59–57.

When Maggie was an underclassman, she wouldn't have grasped the 1-2-2 zone concept. She wouldn't have been able to focus through the anger that would have clouded her vision. As a senior, Maggie knew how to work hard, but more importantly she understood her limits.

It would be a lie to say that Maggie thought I was the perfect coach. I know there were days when she thought I was the world's worst. When Maggie thought I wasn't doing everything possible to help the team win, she let me know in no uncertain terms. Maggie's eyebrow-raising words didn't bother me, partially because I knew she was mad, and teenagers say irrational things when they're mad, but primarily because she and I had different fundamental viewpoints. When she was working, she wanted to win, no exceptions. I, on the other hand, honestly don't care if we win or lose as long as my players understand the life lessons that I think are far more valuable than any statistic.

When I first met Maggie, she had overwhelming self-confidence and didn't understand the importance of being dedicated to both work and play, not getting the two confused, and moving quickly from one to the other. The more she lived the lesson, the more she grasped how to maximize her potential by pursuing her goals with all-out passion, and not mixing work and play.

A couple of weeks after the win over Garfield, I had a conversation with Maggie about her college choices. She was thinking about the University of Washington, but had several other options. I told her about the exceptional qualities of Washington (with a slight bias as I teach there), and she asked if I thought she'd have a chance to make the basketball team. "Maggie, you will be an overwhelming success in whatever you do," I boasted. She gave me her trademark cold stare, but this time there wasn't anger behind it. "I think I will too," she said. "But why do you think I will be?" I smiled and returned her piercing look. "Because you're tremendously smart and you take risks."

"Whether a person is working hard or playing hard, they must take risks," I explained. "Those risks are what allow for amazing success. When you're working, you go crazy to accomplish your mission. When you're playing, you must give just as much effort. And in everything you do, you take those needed risks. Maggie, I have no doubt that you'll be successful."

I smiled as I watched Maggie walk away, wondering if she understood. I bet she did, but it doesn't really matter. Someday she'll realize my prediction was right.

CHAPTER EIGHT

A Lesson for All Parents

Heather, Lindsey, and Bruce Wilson (Photograph courtesy Lindsey Wilson)

this type of parenting approach makes as much sense as hitting a toddler to change her behavior. Anything as important as parenting or teaching life lessons cannot be accomplished with a quick fix. I believe parents are more successful, and actually have much more fun, when they have *preferences* for their child, and banish "expectations" from their parental goals. Over the years, I've coached many players with such parents and they have had noticeably more fun than teenagers who are under constant pressure. For example, a kid does better when her parents prefer she wins a game, but don't expect her to win. And when asked to choose between their child enjoying basketball, or forcing their kid to give up precious teen time to become the state's WNBA draft pick of the year, they'll opt for their kid's overall happiness because they understand the damage of pushing a teen toward fame and fortune. But I can also hear the argument that an athletically gifted girl should be pushed to even further her talent. Alas, there's no good manual to guide us precisely as to where the line is between pursuing sports enjoyment and athletic achievement.

Many coaches I've met opine about how much better the coaching environment was in past decades, when parents were more removed from coaches. Games were more about spirit and fun than winning and losing. Some coaches complain that there is too much emphasis on winning and losing in today's high school sports, and they long for a day when parents don't get involved. I understand their point, but I disagree. I want the families of my athletes to have as much fun as possible and the more they're involved with the Roosevelt basketball team, the more fun will enter their lives. Excluding the over-involved parents I've just mentioned, basketball adds another way for parents to be involved in their teen's life in all the best ways. But there are other benefits—it creates a closer community and provides an arena for parent-to-parent support.

After each Roosevelt season, I hold individual 30-minute meetings with each player and her parents at my home. In addition to the technical basketball information, I tell parents that their daughters are like my own daughters. They're members of my family and I love them, and I want what's best for them. They may not agree with my parenting style, but I'm trying to teach the girls an older perspective in a safe and fun way. I acknowledge to the parents that they may not always agree with my methods. However, when parents disagree, I want them to tell me because they need a place to vent that frustration other than to a spouse or a child. I ask them to e-mail me whenever they have an issue. Maybe I'm inviting the bull into the china shop, but the more I know about parental thoughts, the better job I can do in helping the girls self-govern in a productive and entertaining way.

At my pre-season parent meetings, I spend 15 minutes discussing proper treatment of the referees, and about as much time explaining that after a game, the only thing parents should convey to their daughter is that they're proud of her and that they enjoyed watching her play. After a game, even an all-state player will think of at least 15 things she did wrong, and if a parent is critical of her, it only adds to her self doubts. Instead, if a parent is positive—even if a player is crying—that will bolster her self-esteem.

I explain that parents shouldn't talk to their daughter during the games, but instead let her process her own thoughts. I invite and encourage Roosevelt parents to attend any practices they want, but in most cases they end up not attending any practices. Their daughter will typically tell them they can't come, of course, but it can be helpful. Parents who attend practices see what their daughter goes through as part of the team, and can gain a more complete picture of what their kid is experiencing. The parent meetings are crucial. I have a duty to all the parents to let them know what I think, and to allow them to respond after processing the information. And when overly involved parents act up, I'm right there to discuss it with them.

When I witness an overbearing parent coming down on their child, I'll find a way to have an extra meeting with that parent to explain my observations. "I could be wrong," I say, "but I think you're upsetting your child and I think it'd be better if you to let her handle it. When she comes to you for advice about basketball, probably the best advice you can give her is that she should talk to her coach about it. If that advice doesn't work, then only the parents and coach should converse, and leave the child out of it."

My advice almost never changes the situation. Sometimes the parents refuse to see the problem. Sometimes they just don't want the situation to be fixed.

It's a mystery to me why some parents become hyper-involved and overly intrusive with their child's life, especially when it comes to sports. Unfortunately, this situation happens often enough that I view it as more than a phenomenon. In my first eight years as Roosevelt's head coach, I averaged one or two sets of misbehaved parents per season. But I don't dwell on these outliers. In my experience at Roosevelt, I've been lucky to meet hundreds of model parents who have raised amazing young women and who've even managed to teach me some valuable lessons in the process.

Bruce Wilson, whose daughter Lindsey was an all-state guard in 1999, is an illustrious example of an outstanding parent who "gets it." A star linebacker at Mount Vernon High, Bruce was recruited to the University of Washington, and he was a ferocious athlete during the 1961 season before his football career was cut short due to a back injury. Football players, in any generation, tend to be maniacs, and I couldn't mean that in a more positive way. What makes them good football players is they react quickly, and with rip-your-head-off intensity. Bruce raised his daughter with a linebacker's intensity. To counteract such intensity, his wife, Heather, who almost always carries herself with a broad smile, has a gentle maternal touch that manages to keep Lindsey very well-balanced.

Lindsey wasn't happy at the first high school she attended. Her parents supported her, and transferred her to Roosevelt before her junior year. High school sports regulations forbid me from coaching the team during the spring and fall practice games, so friends in the Roosevelt community take the lead. Since Lindsey transferred to Roosevelt during spring practice games, I wasn't playing an active coaching role but I advised the off-season coaches not to choose Lindsey as one of five starters. I knew that if she *had* started, jealousy from teammates would reach such titanic proportions it would have taken months to overcome—if the team could overcome it at all. The only way the returning Roosevelt players would accept Lindsey as a starter was if they learned through observing her game, and getting on the court with her. Selecting Lindsey as a starter was a decision that would affect the entire team, and the entire season, and so it needed to be a consensus vote amongst the teammates, not a decision made by coaches. When teens are left out of important decisions, they often react in extreme ways. The coaches took my advice. Lindsey's father, Bruce, watched his daughter, one of the best players in Roosevelt history, begin off-season games on the bench. Despite what seemed like a blatant squandering of talent, he never said a word to me about it for months.

Bruce never complained then, or during the regular season when some parents believed he had a right to be bothered with my approach to coaching. His daughter had played basketball eight hours a day since elementary school. She lifted weights daily and did everything imaginable to become the state's best basketball player. Then Lindsey enrolled at Roosevelt and had to report to me, a left-wing liberal coach who didn't play her more than 18 minutes in most games because I didn't want to steamroll opponents. She averaged 22.3 points per game in an average of 18 minutes. Under another coach, Lindsey would have played 30 minutes and could've had a high point-per-game average, which might have shattered state records. Lindsey had that potential and Bruce knew it. But he didn't intrude, or try to influence coaches. He was there for the team, something he would prove time and time again at Lindsey's high school games.

During the regular season of Lindsey's senior year, we faced the Franklin Quakers, her former school. Lindsey sat out with an injury that had kept her sidelined for a few games, and watched as Franklin crept back into a game that earlier had appeared out of reach. Early in the fourth quarter, Bruce came down from the stands and whispered to me, "Do you want me to tell Lindsey to suit up and warm up on the other side of the court where the Franklin girls will see her? It might scare them." It was a perfect idea and far better than my coaching strategy that day.

He told Lindsey she was going into the game. She proceeded to do her full routine of calisthenics and stretches. She put on her usual game face, showing an absolute desire to get in and kill the other team, especially since she'd played with some of the Franklin players and knew their game well. The Quakers' play collapsed with the sight of Lindsey on the sideline. Bruce's plan worked perfectly. Lindsey, however, was infuriated when she found out this was a ruse and she wasn't going in. "What's most important to you?" Bruce asked. "I want to win," she told him. That was why she went through the routine, Bruce explained. "If you knew you weren't going to play, you wouldn't have been as good an actress, and we wouldn't have won the game," he said. As she mulled over the scenario, Lindsey's teenage frustration slowly flowered into a full-on grin. Bruce's approach helped Lindsey learn through her own actions the importance of being a teammate. It's not always your playing on the court that matters.

Another example of Bruce's understanding of what's important came later that season. We had posted a 21–0 record, but in the bi-district championship, Lake Washington pounded us 63–36. *The Seattle Times*, which ranked us as the state's second-best team, said our game suffered from subzero shooting, and they were being kind. I knew I would lose games as a coach, but I didn't want my first loss to be such an out-and-out obliteration. I didn't care about my coaching record—I was frustrated at myself for not finding a way to right the ship and create a better outcome for the players. When it was all over, I mentally replayed the game alone in the stands, too frustrated to talk to anybody. Bruce found me, climbed up the rows, and sat on my right. He captured my eyes with his. "Bill," he said bluntly, but with a grin, "you're fired."

That one sentence put everything in perspective more than any 20-minute pep talk could. We weren't a worse team because we lost. Losing games is a part of life. But I'd lost myself in the moment and forgotten this basic truth to life, until Bruce rallied me together. I appreciate the times when parents reach out to coach me through the rough spots.

In addition to Bruce Wilson, Roosevelt has had so many stellar parents, I could easily write another book recounting all their amazing deeds of collaboration, and I appreciate and thank them all. I regret that the scope of this book allows me to mention only a few out of the many dedicated parents who've graced our hallowed gym.

Ralph Nord, whose daughter Rachel was a senior my first year as head coach, was a concerned dentist who worried that we weren't paying enough attention to the team's medical needs. Instead of complaining, though, Ralph patiently explained his thoughts to me. When I told him I didn't know what to include in the medical kit, he assembled one for the team and declined reimbursement.

Jeff and Erin Argens, parents of 2007 senior Mackenzie Argens, recognized that completing team paperwork was not one of my skills. They organized and founded a group of parents that, through committees, handled myriad duties that I would have spent dozens of hours completing. Though Jeff preferred not to lead the organization, he stepped up when asked to, and Erin chaired a committee that organized a traveling team for summer tournaments. More importantly, Jeff and Erin were always involved in their daughter's academic and basketball careers, but didn't interfere with her development. As a result, they watched Mackenzie develop from a scared freshman to a player who accepted an athletic scholarship to the University of Washington as a junior, while maintaining an honor-roll GPA.

Tom Ostrom volunteered to coach the Roughriders for free during several off-seasons. (High school rules forbade paid basketball coaches from giving off-season instruction.) Tom wasn't a possessive parent who wanted to show up the paid coaching staff. He thought we should run a 1-2-1-1 press, and used his time as volunteer coach to teach it to the team. When some girls didn't run it correctly, he didn't make them run as I might have during the regular season, because Tom knew off-season practices weren't meant to be as intense as regular season practices. And when the paid coaches returned, he didn't insist we keep his choice for a defensive formation. Tom understood that it was the coaches' decision. When we lost crucial games that season, he was always there to tease me, give me five, and thank me for my efforts. Even though his daughter Amanda graduated from Roosevelt in 1999, to this day Tom continues to be a staple in the stands each season. And he still continues to tease me when we lose.

Tammy Hartung was a 2001 graduate who went on to be a Division I college soccer star. She played with us as a freshman and sophomore, but basketball practices were too hard on her ankles. Tammy explained this problem to her parents and they decided she should quit basketball. Tammy's parents told their daughter to leave it up to them—they'd be the ones to break the bad news to Coach Bill. But Tammy told her parents that she'd made the commitment to the team, and it was her responsibility to tell me. And her parents respected their daughter's decision. Faced with this same situation, other parents might have insisted that they break the news to the coach, in order to protect their child from a difficult conversation. But Tammy's parents were exceptional and didn't interfere, allowing their daughter to handle the situation on her own, which created another life experience for Tammy, and another opportunity to grow as a person.

Without the support of dedicated dad Chris Nefcy, I couldn't have helped Angela Nefcy gain confidence in the amazing person that she is. Chris constantly told me what Angela thought of her progress on the basketball court, but just as important was what he told me about the players off the court. Chris was my source for team rumors, which was invaluable information for understanding team chemistry. Over the course of every season, my players get tired of hearing me. They remember the criticisms far more than the compliments, and no matter how young I think I am, there's always a generation gap. Add to that the fact that the girls think I have all the power in the world and it's no surprise they get tired of me late in the season. During the 2000 season when the players had almost hit their boiling point with me, Angela took her dad's suggestion to throw a team bowling party with a therapeutic theme—players who attended were encouraged to let out all their complaints and frustrations about Coach Resler. It gave Angela an opportunity to be a leader, and revived the team camaraderie we needed going into the playoffs.

Craig Watson, the devoted dad of 2001 grad Emily Watson, taught me the concept of parent-style senioritis. The last year of high school comes with hundreds of hurdles—almost all of them as hard on the parents as they can be on kids. Many parents are as eager to taste the freedom they'll enjoy with the kids away at college as much as the teens want to fly the coop and experience life on their own. During Emily's senior year, Craig told me he felt overly anxious about how his family life would change when his daughter went away to college. It was hard for him to relax and enjoy some of her senior games, especially given these would be her last high school games. After Emily graduated, Craig still came to our games and confessed that it was much more fun. None of my daughters competed in high school athletics, so I had no idea that the parents may come down with their own case of senioritis. It was a lesson I learned from a parent coaching me, and one I use when dealing with parents of seniors each season when their desire for winning is highly accentuated.

Some parents also understand that my role as coach can extend far beyond the courts. Emily Johnson, whose daughter Laura Mohler was a sophomore on our 2004 state championship team, invited me to her home during the off-season to discuss academics with her daughter. For as long as she could remember, Laura loved basketball. But Laura was a typical teen—she didn't love her homework. Laura's mom explained to me that if her daughter's grade point average didn't improve, she wouldn't allow her to play basketball. Emily could have enforced this rule herself, but felt it important that I be involved for additional support. I love that Emily believed that school was more important than basketball, and that she knew that the Roosevelt community would do anything to help a fellow Roughrider. Laura heard from both her mom and me that school is the most important aspect of her life. Emily's plan worked: Laura transferred her basketball intensity to the classroom and earned a 4.0 GPA as a junior. That grade point and work ethic paid off, and Laura accepted an academic scholarship from California's Occidental College, where she continued studying hard and playing basketball.

Of all the extraordinary parent-child stories, though, my favorite is that of Dino Nims and Piper. I've always felt that his relationship with his daughter, a 2000 Roosevelt graduate, was as close and loving as any parent-child relationship I've ever witnessed. Dino told me that on one occasion when Piper was in fifth grade she wanted to play hoops with her dad. But Dino was napping and too exhausted to get up. "Go paint my car," he told her. Following dad's instructions, dutiful daughter Piper headed to the garage where she gathered up several colors of leftover house paint, and went to task, painting polka dots, squiggles, spirals, and stars on every panel of the family car. Dino never got mad. He was as proud as he'd ever been, and drove his car like that for years. From Dino's point of view, Piper's painting was a badge of honor that showed off how creative his daughter was.

Dino was very laid-back, and always up for a good laugh. He sat in the very last row at all games so he was free to do his Dino thing, being as obnoxious as he wanted without bothering people. When the game was over, he was happy-go-lucky whether we won or lost. Whenever

he had a criticism of Roosevelt coaches—usually about game strategy—he waited two or three days before bringing it up to make sure
it was a valid issue. In many ways, Dino was a dream parent.

In Piper's senior season, Dino contracted an extended illness
that kept him bedridden for months. Doctors told him he wouldn't
be able to attend any of Piper's games, but there was no way Dino
was going to miss watching his daughter play. Dino exceeded every
doctor's expectation the night he walked to the final row of the
Roosevelt bleachers to watch us play a late-season game against our
rival Redmond. Unfortunately, we weren't as happy with the final
score as we were with Dino's arrival. The Mustangs destroyed us
53–31. When the game mercifully ended, still-weak Dino strolled
across the hardwood and with a smile said, "I got out of bed for this
(bleep)?" It was the first time I'd laughed since the final buzzer. Even
in the direst situations, Dino knew how to have fun. In his strange
Dino way, his knowledge of basketball and sense of humor helped
Piper and me enjoy several hoop seasons.

At every coaching conference I've been to, the most common conversations aren't about Xs and Os or how to teach pick-and-rolls.
Coaches want to talk about how to deal with parents. The discussion
usually turns into coaches trading war stories, with each ensuing
story starting with, "Oh, you think that was bad? Listen to this . . ."
Coaches share horror stories of lawsuits, and parents flying out of
the stands to punch them in the nose. I'm convinced that any high
school coach with a year of experience has dealt with at least one
major parent-induced blowout. It's a fine feeling to observe excellent parenting. That joy, however, is overshadowed by the pain of
witnessing an unruly parent ruining his or her daughter's experience. Of course, misbehaving parents never see their actions as a
major part of the problem. Instead, they always shift the blame to
someone besides themselves.

In 1992 when I was coaching an American Athletic Union (AAU) team, I cut a girl after tryouts partly because she wasn't the same age as the other players, but primarily because she wasn't aggressive enough on the court. To be a basketball player you *have* to exhibit aggression, and this girl didn't show even a trace of aggression. I knew letting her go was the correct decision, but my decision didn't sit well at all with the girl's mother.

Five years later I became the Roosevelt head coach, and it was then that I learned how long an angry parent can hold a grudge. Other parents told me that the mother of the girl I'd cut five years earlier was telling anyone who would listen that I hated her daughter and was trying to ruin their family. I hadn't thought about that player in years, but other parents in the Roosevelt community told me that this myopic mother was convinced I'd systematically set out to destroy her child's future by cutting her from the team when she was in fifth grade. The mother undoubtedly had tremendous love for her daughter, but she wasn't being realistic. This mother didn't know when to step back, and the outspoken manner she used in order to benefit her daughter only harmed her child in the long run.

When she got to Roosevelt, the girl I'd cut at AAU tryouts turned out for hoops and made the junior varsity as a freshman. Her mother, however, was livid because she believed her daughter had what it takes to become one of the best players on the varsity squad. The girl wasn't a bad player, but other Roosevelt players were quicker and far more aggressive.

By the time the same girl entered her senior season, in my opinion she was the eighth- or ninth-best player in the varsity program. But her mother refused to believe she was anything but the best. She told dozens of other Roosevelt parents that her daughter would definitely be a Division I college basketball player, and complained that I was attempting to ruin her daughter's life by limiting her playing time.

To ease this burden a little, I started the girl in 18 regular season games, prompting a teammate to jokingly say, "I wish my mom would go yell at Bill, so I could start every game." One of those games was a buzzer-beater, and I didn't play her in the final few minutes because I didn't think she was the correct fit in a pressure situation. After the game, the mother and daughter pulled me aside to complain that I didn't respect the girl, and didn't treat her as the awesome star that she was. I told them that I greatly respected the girl, but that I pulled her out of the game because I believed we'd have a better chance to win with other players. This message was lost on the girl and her mom, who seemed to loathe me more with each word I spoke. It's been my experience that most other parents are able to rethink their positions, and realize that their expectations are unreasonable.

I've come to learn that just about all parents who lose control start with the same phrase: "I promised myself I wasn't going to be the parent who would interfere. But . . ." Then they launch forth. In this case, the mom didn't waste time with the introduction. She wrote inflammatory outlandish letters to the principal and openly spoke to all within earshot about what an awful person I was.

Things reached an all-time low weeks later, when her daughter went to the Roosevelt principal and claimed that one of my assistants groped her. The claim was completely bogus, but the severity of the accusation meant that he would be fired immediately and I would likely follow. Other girls on the team got word of what happened, and unbeknownst to me went to the Roosevelt principal, explaining the situation and claiming that the allegations were lies.

The girls later recalled the scene to me. The principal asked them to give their counter-accusations the careful thought that such a weighty situation requires. "Let's suppose ten years go by and you find out that the assistant coach really was doing these things," he asked them. "Is this a case where you'd look back and think maybe there were some signs, but you just didn't recognize them at the time?" I'm glad the principal was so thorough. If I were in his shoes, I would have to see overwhelming evidence not to fire the coaches. The girls' defense was resolute, though. I didn't know until an investigation cleared all coaches of wrongdoing that those girls had testified on my assistant coach's behalf. Without them, who knows what would have happened.

The incident frightens me in terms of how far some parents are willing to go when their daughter doesn't get what they think she deserves. Sadly, when parents lose control they transfer their anger and frustrations to the coaches and believe it is the coaches who have gone mad. And some parents take it all the way—they'll stop at nothing to get coaches fired.

In the summer, Roosevelt hosts hoop camps for grade school and middle school girls. Some girls attend hoop camp from grade school until they're old enough to enroll at Roosevelt, and start bleeding green and yellow (our school colors) in the process. At these camps, the girls get hours of encouragement from my coaching staff and the high school players who coach the youngsters. We do our best to make them believe in themselves and inspire them to set high goals. Unfortunately for some who dream of being Roughriders, their dreams turn to heartache when they don't make varsity. When this occurs, the majority of parents console their daughters, and find ways to teach their kids how to get through and learn from life's more challenging experiences.

One of the toughest situations I've faced as a coach involved a shy girl who participated in hoop camp for six years. When a pass came her way, she ducked. When she needed to take a charge, she ran the other way. But something extraordinary occurred during the girl's seventh-grade camp championship. From out of nowhere, this same, shy, right-handed girl drove with her left hand and sank the shot—I was thoroughly impressed. The moment was out of character for her, and was a perfect example to refer to when she needed encouragement. "That shot was nails!" I told her. "You just hammered that home!"

Despite such encouragement, she was so timid when she tried out at Roosevelt her freshman year that we almost cut her. We kept her on the JVC out of loyalty since she'd attended hoop camp for so many years, but we knew that she wouldn't make the varsity unless she got a major aggression-injection. Rather than being supportive and realistic, the girl's dad complained to every Roosevelt coach that his daughter should have made the JV team.

Halfway through that season, the JVC coach quit and the Roosevelt athletic director was thrown into the coaching role. Most parents understood that the director was just filling in and didn't fully know the team personnel. Those parents also realized that the point of these games was for the girls to have fun while improving their skills. But this girl's father was the outlier. When he didn't like a decision, he climbed down from the stands and screamed at the substitute JVC coach in front of the teenagers and fellow parents. He was a textbook example of what not to do as a parent. It was an embarrassing situation. Not even a five-year-old should behave that way, let alone a parent.

In her sophomore year, the overly passive girl came to all eight weekly summer practices. But unlike Angela Nefcy (see Chapter 5), the only other player who attended all eight practices, the taciturn girl didn't constantly push herself. Whenever I watched her walk through drills, I wondered whether she was there because she wanted to be there, or because she was forced to be there by a parent who was trying to live through her. The Roosevelt coaches still knew she wasn't likely to be a varsity athlete with her timid court demeanor and 5-foot-4 frame, but we put her on the JV because she'd been so dedicated during the summer.

Attempting to avoid a disaster, I told the Roosevelt athletic director that we needed to have a meeting with the girl's parents and the junior varsity coach to explain our observations. I knew that the girl probably wouldn't make varsity the following year and I didn't want her or her parents to be blindsided.

During the meeting in a Roosevelt conference room, the parents were asked what their goals were for their daughter. "I'm hoping that when she plays for the varsity, she'll break Roosevelt's record for 3-point shooting percentage," her dad said. Not only was that ridiculously unrealistic, that was a stat we don't even record. I carefully explained that we don't worry about statistics like that, and instead we focus on the interpersonal development of the players. "Well," he snapped, "we want her to be a star shooter on the varsity."

Over the course of the meeting, the coaches explained to the parents that their daughter would never make the varsity unless she became aggressive, which was the key to being successful. I expressed my doubts as to whether she would ever develop the athletic attitude. When we talked, it seemed as though my words hit the parents' foreheads and dropped to the table. In the weeks after the meeting, I sat next to the girl's dad at JV games and pointed out his daughter's mistakes so he could understand where she needed improvement. But he refused to see what was obvious.

During the summer before his daughter's junior year, two Canadian girls transferred so they could play on our team. Eligibility rules required them to play with the junior varsity for a year, but the father who wanted his daughter to set the 3-point record was convinced that the Canadian girls were recruited in order to keep his daughter off of varsity. He was so convinced of his conspiracy theory, he launched a campaign against the Roosevelt coaching staff. On an almost daily basis, this misguided father called and wrote complaints to the Washington Interscholastic Activities Association, the Roosevelt principal, and the Seattle School District. To no coach's surprise, his daughter quit basketball amidst all this turmoil.

This conspiracy-theorist dad was so infuriated he created a Web site that bashed the Roosevelt coaches, and he posted evidence to support his theory that the Canadian players didn't belong at Roosevelt. He posted uncensored rants against me, explaining in vivid detail why he thought I was a worthless person, and why I needed to be fired. Thankfully, the Seattle School District realized he was just another enraged parent gone wild and to my knowledge didn't waste money on an investigation. Two years after his tirade meant to get the Roosevelt coaching staff fired, we won the school's first state championship.

What did his daughter learn from her father's reactions, and actions? She learned to point fingers when she didn't get her way. This father didn't teach his daughter to own her own life; he taught her that other people were to blame for her own shortcomings. I wonder how much better her game would've been if her father had been realistic and supportive of his daughter's desires.

My experiences are just the tip of the iceberg when it comes to sad stories involving irrational parents. Karen Blair, who I feel is one of Washington State's all-time best high school coaches, took her Meadowdale High team to the state tournament ten out of her eleven years at the school, winning the Class 3A title in 2000 and 2004. But three months after her team's tenth state berth, Blair resigned, citing frustration over a few critical parents that wouldn't talk to her face-to-face, but had no problem tattling to the school district. Her resignation produced an outcry from former players and parents who held a rally at the school, but the damage was already done. After resigning from Meadowdale, she coached at Ballard High in Seattle where she led the Beavers to a 12–11 record—the school's best in more than a decade.

In 2006, a 24-year-old boys basketball coach at Seattle's Chief Sealth High became the target of vandals, who slashed his car tires not once, but twice during a season when at least one parent went behind his back to undermine him. In February 2005, Seattle news stations led their broadcasts with a video of an enraged Gig Harbor parent punching his daughter's basketball coach in the face after her team lost a playoff game 56–41.

Potential problems exist for every high school team. But what makes me want to be a high school coach is the potential for positive experiences that can help teenagers turn into compassionate, understanding adults. I want each of my players to graduate high school with a strong decision-making ability, coupled with a healthy notion of what's right and wrong. The girls should have a strong sense of personal and team responsibility, and at the end of the day, they should come away with a joyful, exuberant feeling about basketball. They should share concerns about humanity and our environment. I also hope they desire to have as much fun as possible in a lifetime of learning. It's unlikely that all of these skills will be in place at age 18, but it is a worthy goal.

Parents who can step back and let their teenagers develop through their own experiences have taken a Goliath step toward implementing these goals. But for some reason, there will always be parents who can't step back, and this is one of the major reasons I created the Inner Circle for my players. The Inner Circle is for players only, and it's designed to shut out those parents who don't realize that life and basketball should be as fun as possible and that their daughters' game is not about the parents' expectations.

When teenagers experience problems, they often feel that the problem is much larger than it actually is. The issue of whether a parent should support their children or whether they should let their children handle the problem on their own is more a metaphysical choice than a scientific principle. As parents, teachers, and coaches, we often guess in this shadowy setting. My coaching philosophy errs on the side of giving kids more power, but always keeping the lines of communication open. As adults, there are thousands of lessons we can learn from kids, too. I believe there are two primary directions on the basketball court of life. When we give our kids freedom to make their own choices, we set them on a course to becoming responsible, goal-oriented adults. And when adults take this approach, we also end up learning a lot about life.

CHAPTER NINE

Betty Harris

Betty Harris, wearing her daughter Emiko's letterman jacket (Photograph by Casey McNerthney)

Inch by Inch

There's a lesson I repeat so often that my players start mocking me before I can finish it: "Inch by inch, life's a cinch. Yard by yard, life is hard." Some think it's goofy, but I think it's an invaluable lesson for teenagers who can easily get caught up in worrying about the final conclusion instead of the little things that must be done to reach a goal.

If players focus on the state tournament at the start of the season, their far-sighted focus may lose the regular season's games they must win to qualify for state. When underclassmen only focus on the vast difference in talent and skill between themselves and the top varsity players, they lose sight of the fact that their skills will improve through dedicated daily effort. On and off the court, I believe the most effective way for people to overcome challenges is by working through them inch by inch.

I've watched many players embody this lesson and use it to better themselves as basketball players. But our basketball players aren't the only people in the Roosevelt community who have exemplified the life lessons. While the Inner Circle is the true team, I think the parents and their experiences are as important as the players on the court. In the previous chapter, I related a few stories of key individual parents who understood the value of the game and the lessons I teach. There are several parents who have lived the lessons I try to convey, and have taught others more through their experience than I could ever teach in a practice. This chapter is about one of those parents.

Betty Harris, whose daughter Emiko graduated in 2003, understands the importance of the inch-by-inch lesson better than anyone I've known. She didn't initially make friends with other Roosevelt parents, but every time she walked into the gym, she exuded an unconditional love that soon made others love her back. And when Betty's life was hard, members of the Roosevelt family helped her inch along.

Betty's boundless support for her daughter was the first thing I noticed when I met her in the summer of 2000. Emiko was a freshman on the JV that year, and no matter who we were playing, I could always count on Betty to be cheering with a rich laugh and a voice that could be heard two states away, regardless of the score.

Her love and support for her daughter was also obvious during the only confrontation Betty had with me, though it came in a form not obvious to everyone. Between Emiko's freshman and sophomore years, we played in the championship of a summer basketball tournament, and the game came down to the final minute. Emiko was still a member of the JV and I didn't think she had enough experience to handle the pressure situation, so I didn't play her for a second.

Betty approached me near the scorers table after the game. She was smiling, but her face showed that she had come to me with a purpose. She skipped the small talk and asked me point-blank why I didn't play her daughter. I gave her my assessment of Emiko's talent and said she wasn't yet ready to play in the final minute of a close championship game. Betty eyed me for a few seconds and asked, "Is the reason you didn't play her because she's black?"

I was stunned by the accusation because a player's race has never affected who I play. I was even more confused because Darnellia Russell, another black guard, had played nearly the entire game.

When I pointed out Darnellia's playing time, Betty responded, "Yes, but you treat her like she's a white girl."

Despite her playing the race card, the lawyer in me was impressed that she had retorted with an answer that left me silent and without an immediate answer. Honestly I wasn't upset or offended by that racial accusation, as I knew she was just talking in the heat of the moment. I have seen the race card played in nasty confrontational settings, but this wasn't even close to that case. I knew that the only reason she accused me was she didn't want anyone mistreating her baby. Today, after all we've been through together, Betty and I laugh about that early conversation.

Betty, who was born and raised in Louisiana, saw herself as a country girl. She offered no pretense in interactions and was proud to be her loud, loving self regardless of the funny looks she sometimes got from other parents. To this day, whenever I see Betty at the gym, her greeting is more reliable than taxes. "Heeyyyyyy Bill!" she'll yell before running down to give me a maternal bear hug. "I'm so excited to see you!"

She's the kind of woman who doesn't waste time with a handshake—she greets friends with hugs. And once Betty befriends someone, she's on call for that person for the rest of their life. Generous-hearted Betty remembers birthdays and calls friends out of the blue to remind them that they're special. When players make mistakes on the court, Betty knows they feel devastated and is there to pick them up. From her usual spot in the third row of the Roosevelt bleachers she'll call out, "It's OK! You're fine, baby, you're fine."

Betty came to Seattle from New Orleans in 1988 so her mom could get special treatment at Harborview Medical Center for a life-threatening illness. Her mother died in 1992, but Betty stayed in Seattle to keep her three children with the friends they had grown up with.

Betty raised her kids near Garfield High in Seattle's Central District. But she sent them seven miles up the road to Roosevelt, which was predominantly filled with middle- and upper-class white kids. Betty did this because she wanted her kids to stay in school, and stay away from the temptations that were part of their lower-income part of town.

Her neighbors and friends—many of whom graduated from Garfield—didn't let a week go by without bragging about the Garfield Bulldogs. Whenever Garfield beat us, Betty had to go to a grocery store in another neighborhood instead of going to the one walking distance from her home. If she had, she would have gotten more "Go Bulldogs" comments than groceries. But when the Roughriders won, she would proudly wear Emiko's letterman jacket everywhere—even when hot weather made it impractical.

As a freshman and sophomore Emiko was quiet, though she always laughed at the outrageous behavior of the older girls on the team. She swung between the junior varsity and varsity as a junior, getting most of her varsity minutes in blowouts. As a 5-foot-6 senior, she contributed a team-high 14 points in a 58–55 season-opening win against a strong Enumclaw team. Later that year, she dropped in another team-high 14 in a fist-clenching 48–47 win against Lake Washington. Betty was there in the third row for every inch of Emiko's basketball career, cheering louder than anyone else.

Other parents were more reserved, and as such didn't immediately form a bond with Betty. But instead of worrying that she may be a parental outsider for all of Emiko's four years, she focused only on each day, each step in the long journey of life. During varsity games, she would sit with Emiko's JV friends, who warmed up to Betty's bear hugs from the first week.

The bridge between Betty and the Roosevelt parents was Silas Wild, father of Jenny Wild who was a year older than Emiko. Betty can't remember exactly what game it was when Silas started a conversation with her, but she remembers how comfortable he made her feel. They talked about their kids and the team and the season and all the little things that made Betty feel like she belonged. "You're kinda cool," Betty recalled telling him. "Let me show you the black handshake." And from that day forward, Betty sat with Silas and his wife at almost every game. Inch by inch, the other parents started to realize how dynamic this mom was with her wild cackling laugh and amazing ability to stir up the players with boisterous yells of encouragement.

But the moment that made her understand she would always be a loved member of the Roosevelt family came from one of Emiko's teammates. Leyla Khastou, who was a freshman on the JVC team during Emiko's sophomore year, was given an assignment in her English class to write a biography of someone she respected, someone who was inspirational, someone who she was glad to know. Betty said the day Leyla told her she wrote about her was one of the best days of her life. "She could have written about a whole bunch of people," Betty recalled, choking up at the recollection. "And here's this little white girl writing about me."

Betty worked as a nurse's aide at Bailey-Boushay House—a residential care and day health center for AIDS patients—and later at Harborview Medical Center. She said she chose the profession because she's always been a giver. She was always the one who wanted to boost others' self-esteem. And though she knew dozens of her patients by name and cared about them like they were family, it was her true family she cared about most. That's why she told co-workers she had to move back to New Orleans, to be near Emiko when she attended Xavier University in 2003. Though Betty's close friends and well-paying job were in Seattle, she was a dedicated single parent who didn't want to send her love over the telephone.

Betty arrived in New Orleans a few months after Emiko's spring graduation and she immediately felt at home. Her dad was there, as was her mom's only living sister and dozens of cousins. She was living a few miles from L. W. Higgins High, where she'd graduated in 1980 after her tenure as a varsity basketball forward. Back in 2001, the year her oldest daughter enrolled at Xavier, Betty bought a house in New Orleans's West Bank region. As a kid, she had lived in the West Bank—located across the Mississippi River from New

Orleans's central business district. She had survived many unnerving hurricane seasons, and when she moved back she said she wasn't scared of surviving another one.

Betty first heard about Hurricane Katrina on August 24, 2005—the day after it formed over the Bahamas. She didn't follow the news reports very closely, as Katrina crossed southern Florida as a moderate Category 1 hurricane, or as the storm gained strength in the Gulf of Mexico. Betty, who'd lived through more hurricanes in one season than most do in a lifetime, was sure it would turn away from New Orleans, or at least weaken if it did hit. She'd already survived Hurricane Cindy and Hurricane Dennis earlier that year. Hurricane Katrina wouldn't be different, she thought.

But daughter Emiko was terrified by news reports predicting it could be the deadliest hurricane in U.S. history. She begged her mom to leave the house, still boarded up from Hurricane Dennis, which tore through New Orleans the previous month. Betty tried to calm her daughter's fears early on the afternoon of August 28, but when newscasters reported that all roads leading out of the city would be shut down at 6 p.m., other relatives started to worry.

So Betty followed Emiko, two cousins, a niece, and Emiko's friend into the family's Lincoln Navigator. Betty didn't pack any photo albums or business papers. The only possessions she brought were a toothbrush and three days' worth of clothes. She was sure they'd be back before they ran out of supplies. But a few minutes into the race out of New Orleans, Betty shrieked and demanded that they return to their potentially doomed home.

"We have to go back!" she yelled. "We *have* to go back." Emiko thought her mom was acting crazy. Few things were worth the risk and worth the lost time in already-deadlocked traffic. But Betty didn't stop yelling until the car stopped and turned back to their house. She ripped the boards off of an entrance, ran to her room and took down

Emiko's Roosevelt letterman's jacket, which she'd proudly hung on her bedroom wall. Only when Betty had slipped into the beloved jacket did she finally feel secure.

The family drove more than 300 miles to Columbus, Mississippi, and though they found a shelter sometime after midnight, not one of them slept. They suffered through intense rain and wind with no power, but worse was the fear of not knowing what would happen. Betty had been hesitant to leave New Orleans because of the economic hit it had on her pocketbook—she'd already spent her entire savings on that month's bills and Emiko's college tuition payment. By the time Betty fled on August 28, she and her family were living on credit cards.

She later told me the worst part of the ordeal was not knowing what would happen. Except for Emiko's Roosevelt letterman's jacket, Betty had left behind all of her valuables and hadn't packed enough clothes for what was turning into a devastating state of emergency back in New Orleans. Much worse than her clothes or valuables, Betty had no idea where her brother or father were.

She knew she'd be overcome with grief if she worried about where they may be a week, a month, a year later. Who knew when she'd even be able to return to New Orleans, or find out if her property had suffered damage? And worrying over the fates of family and friends was more than she could bear. She saw panic in the faces at the shelter, hundreds of people who wondered how and even if they'd survive. But Betty didn't focus on the long term. Instead, she only focused on what she was doing each day, each hour, each minute to take care of her family. If her family progressed inch by inch, Betty knew they would eventually recover.

During the first week of September, Betty and Emiko traveled to Port Arthur, Texas, in search of relatives, and found shelter at the Ford Center. It was a world Betty had never imagined—living like a refugee with an identification bracelet in a homeless shelter. "You hear about natural disasters, but you never expect to find yourself in the middle of one," she told me. "I'm a strong person, so I stayed strong for the family. I just wanted everybody to be happy and think positive, but inside I was thinking, 'Oh, God.'"

Betty didn't make plans for things she couldn't control; she confronted the obstacles that appeared in front of her, inch by inch. To pass time, she read stories to the kids who were staying at the shelter. She showed them how to spell their names, taught them to count and recite the alphabet. Although they were going through what was likely the worst tragedy of their lives, they were still kids with the desire to learn and the need to be happy, she said.

Betty had almost nothing, but she did have her family and the security of Emiko's letterman's jacket. "I wore that jacket every day," Betty said. "I was burning up in that jacket, but I just had to wear it."

She thought about her dad every hour after the hurricane and wished she cold see him alive again. Though uncertainty led to almost-unbearable heartache, Betty stayed focused on her family's survival in Port Arthur, and prayed that her inch-by-inch method would lead to a positive outcome.

One afternoon at the Ford Center, Betty sat next to a man reading a local newspaper, and screamed when she saw an article's picture. The newspaper had a picture of her dad and told how the 83-year-old survived Katrina by hitchhiking to McKinney, Texas, with nothing but the clothes on his back. Betty used phones at the Ford Center to contact her dad at a McKinney shelter, got directions and a rental car, and after a six-hour drive, father and daughter were reunited.

Later that week, Betty got a call from her missing brother, saying he was alive and safe in Georgia. "Every day was a step," she said. "I just took it one day at a time and asked God to carry me through."

Industrious Betty used Ford Center fax machines to send Emiko's transcript to Holy Names University, a Jesuit university in Oakland, California, affiliated with Xavier. When Holy Names accepted Emiko for temporary placement, Betty used a credit card to fly her youngest daughter to the next inch of her forward-moving journey.

Betty traveled to Beaumont, Texas, hoping to find shelter with her distant cousin. Though the Internet and the local phone book provided no leads, Betty pressed on, asking anyone who would listen if they knew the kind, petite woman she was related to. At a church dinner, someone did, and drove Betty to the home of her cousin, who immediately welcomed her.

In mid-September, Betty was allowed back into New Orleans's West Bank, which had fared better than downtown New Orleans. Wind had knocked a tree through the roof of her three-bedroom house and rain damage had been caused from the hole it created. But her most important possessions—photo albums, her daughter's diploma, business papers, and family heirlooms—were saved.

Joined by her sister, Betty retuned to her cousin's home in Beaumont, but stayed less than two weeks. On September 24, Hurricane Rita made landfall near the Texas-Louisiana border as a Category 3 hurricane. About a month after fleeing New Orleans from Hurricane Katrina, Betty had to run again.

Staying in a shelter, away from her kids (who are her best friends), Betty said it was at this point when she finally felt completely devastated. She had done all she could, battling inch by inch to survive, and still the odds seemed overwhelming. Again, she prayed for strength and for something to get her through the next inch of her journey. With the devastation in New Orleans, Betty longed to return to Seattle, the only place besides New Orleans where she felt at home. She had friends in Seattle, knew the nooks of the city, and wanted the security of familiar settings.

To this day, Betty swears the woman who approached her in a Beaumont shelter was an angel. She asked Betty where she lived, and how she'd fared through the weeks after Katrina. The kind stranger showed genuine concern when Betty told her she wanted to go back to Seattle but couldn't pay for a plane ticket because she'd maxed out her credit cards helping her children.

"You're obviously a loving mother," the woman said, hearing Betty praise her children. The woman was with the Episcopalian church and she connected Betty with another parishioner, who bought her a plane ticket to Seattle. "When you get there, go to St.

Mark's Episcopal Cathedral," the woman said. "They'll be expecting you on the next step of your journey."

Betty called St. Mark's Episcopal Cathedral the day she touched down in Seattle, and the parishioners immediately gave her shelter. They didn't see it as taking in a stranger—the parishioners who helped Betty saw her as a friend in need. They arranged a home for her in a basement apartment, and gave her money for clothes and meals she couldn't afford to provide for herself.

Friends of Betty who had worked with her at Harborview had searched for their New Orleans girl on the Internet after Hurricane Katrina. When they finally tracked Betty down, they promised to help Betty get a job if she returned to Seattle. When she needed them, they kept their promise. Betty has told me that some went as high as the medical center's CEO to tell him how valuable she was as a worker, and how they needed to help her after what she'd been through. During her first days back, the staff welcomed her with a party that lined a conference room with food. They gave her much-needed gift cards to help her get back on her feet, and many gave her new nursing scrubs because, even though she wasn't required to wear them, Betty always insisted on coming to work in scrubs.

Betty isn't the sort of person who seeks out pity. She's the type who has a hard time just asking for help. As she tried to get her life back to normal after Katrina, only people in Betty's Inner Circle really knew about her struggles and the heartache she continued to face with her temporary living situation.

Later that year, Betty began renting a one-bedroom apartment in West Seattle. One of her first friends to visit was Ward Serrill, the filmmaker of *The Heart of the Game*. When he visited Betty she had only a mattress—bought for her by a friend from Harborview—a wooden chair, and a TV donated by other work friends. But Ward didn't care about material things; he cared about Betty, whom he loved like any one of his family members. They talked for hours about everything, especially about Roosevelt basketball, and what had happened to the team during the years she'd been gone.

"I kept a lot of things hidden within," Betty said. "I didn't want to show too much emotion because I'm the strong one in the family. But with Ward, it was easy. He was the connection between me and Roosevelt."

He showed her clips of the documentary, and reminded her of the fun times she and other Roosevelt parents had. Betty was the same loving person she'd always been, but it was clear she was suffering. She told Ward that what she really wanted was a sofa sleeper so when her kids came to visit, they could have their own bed. He told Betty not to worry. She would have what she needed soon.

Ward called me after leaving Betty's apartment and told me about her condition. He knew it would be hard for her to accept help, but we had a duty to help one of our own. That week, Roosevelt had a potluck dinner at the school for the start of the basketball season. It's a tradition I started in my first year as head coach as a way for the parents and coaches to feel more like the extended family that we are. After dinner, I explained Betty's connection to Roosevelt and told of her need. Though many had never met Betty, there wasn't a parent there who didn't immediately want to help.

Mary Jean Ryan, mother of 2005–06 freshman Rachel Bollens, jumped in to spearhead the efforts. She contacted Betty and got a list of things she needed, and put the word out to other Roosevelt parents. Some people sent checks the day they got Mary Jean's e-mail. Others went to the mall to buy pots and pans, new sheets, green and yellow towels—anything that would make Betty's apartment feel like home. A friend from Mary Jean's work donated a brown sofa sleeper, which Betty adorned with stuffed animals for Emiko.

"I'm the giver," Betty said. "I'm the one who always wanted to boost up people's self-esteem. When I was on that side [being a receiver instead of a giver], it was hard. But I felt so loved."

Though she often felt too sad and traumatized to leave her own house, Betty sporadically attended Roosevelt games in the 2005–06 season, which began less than four months after Hurricane Katrina. She hadn't lost any of her Roughrider spirit. Parents wanted to give more than just that one week of support to someone who had supported so many just by being herself. I always felt relieved to see Betty in the stands because she was the kind of ideal, supportive parent that every coach hopes for. I know her spirit made Roosevelt girls be much better teammates, and more important she helped them become better people. Dozens of other Roosevelt fans felt the same, and we knew it would help her spirit if we showed her how much we loved her.

Emiko visited Betty in Seattle during her 2006 winter break and invited her mom to watch us play in our annual holiday basketball tournament. Emiko, who was part of the plan to get Betty to the gym that night, didn't let on to her mother that this game would hold a surprise for Betty. But Betty didn't need much convincing—she was ready, willing, and able to yell her support for the Roughriders.

At halftime, I grabbed the announcer's microphone and talked about a certain fan who had inspired hundreds in the Roosevelt family. I glanced at Betty, who had no idea what was coming.

"Betty Harris has been there for the Roughriders every time we needed support," I said, inviting her down to the court. As the parents gave her a standing applause, I handed Betty her Fan of the Decade award and her green and yellow lifetime pass to all Roosevelt home games. "Inch by inch, Betty's support helped us become a better team," I said. "And more importantly, she helped us become better people."

Later that season, I loved sharing each of our victories with Betty in the stands as much as I did with my players on the courts. And because of her enduring spirit, I'm sure she'll be there with bear hugs and heartfelt cheers for years to come. Roosevelt basketball is a family far more than it is a team. While players may graduate from Roosevelt High School, they and their families never graduate from the Roosevelt basketball family.

After Betty escaped Hurricane Katrina, when she was living like a ref-ugee hundreds of miles from her home, not knowing if her loved ones were alive, she focused on what she could control that day, and what she could do that moment to make her loved ones happy. Because she focused on the obstacles she could control, one at a time, she per-severed in a life-threatening situation and thrived with the support of those who loved her. When she returned to Seattle with almost no possessions, she employed the same tactic, concentrating on what needed to be done now and on moving forward, day by day.

Had she worried about the bigger picture and not focused on taking small steps, Betty would have been overwhelmed. Had Betty been consumed with worries of her overall journey, she may not have had the conversation with the women who located her cousin in Beaumont. She could have easily missed the newspaper picture that led her to her dad. I'm sure it was Betty's inch-by-inch attitude that allowed her to survive a catastrophe that could have ruined her and her loved one's lives.

Every time my players hear me repeat the "inch-by-inch" lesson, they mock me before I can finish. But after they hear Betty's story, they understand it.

The "inch-by-inch" lesson applies to each individual on the team, and to the collective group. It helps teach the very fundamen-tals of practice. I tell my players to focus on each practice session, and not to think about upcoming games or the season. I even design practices so drills are run in short increments, often five minutes long. I keep drills short so players give all-out effort for every second of those five minutes, then move on to the next practice segment. Each individual gives as much as she can by living in the moment, and the team proceeds through practices inch by inch. They don't worry about how each drill will make them better players over time—the players understand they'll improve overall by focusing on each immediate challenge in front of them.

As the game season gets under way, I build on the inch-by-inch concept during games. I don't want my players focusing on what direction a game is going, or where they'd be in the rankings if they won or lost a particular game. That's too much of a distraction. Instead, I want them focused on each play, and what they need to do to overcome each obstacle that gets in their way. It's that kind of play-by-play focus that drives a winning team.

During the aftermath of Hurricane Katrina, Betty Harris didn't worry about how she'd survive in the long run—she knew she would thrive if she focused on the challenges as they came. Instead of worrying about what she couldn't control, she dealt with challenges on a day-to-day basis and had faith that she'd survive, and thrive. If you survive through each of the five-minute obstacles—in basketball and in life—those small successes will lead to even greater ones.

CHAPTER TEN

Darnellia Russell

Darnellia Russell (Photograph by Casey McNerthney)

Never Give Up

Every high school basketball coach I know has stories about *that one player*. Some tell stories of the all-state guard who grabbed a rebound and led her team to victory in a game many newspaper reporters predicted they'd lose. I've heard of many players from disadvantaged homes who tread steadfastly through acres of adversity and achieved goals that never appeared on a scoreboard. These stand-out players may differ in backgrounds, personalities, and many other ways, but in all of the stories I've heard there's always one constant, one thing they share in common. Through their overall essence and their actions on and off the court, they create life-changing moments for their coaches. From the second they enter the gym for the first time, it's clear that they're different from anyone else you've met, or anyone else you will meet.

If you've read all of the stories in this book, by now you know I've been one lucky coach. I was lucky to coach Lindsey Wilson, who reaffirmed to me why it's important to share your talents. Then there was Alaina Forbes, who taught me more about human spirit and the will to achieve than anyone I've ever met. Angela Nefcy proved the value of owning your own life. In the years I've been coaching, I've met dozens of compelling characters who have taught me far more than I could teach them. But as incredible as those young women were in my life, Darnellia Russell will probably always be the player who stands out the most in my lifetime.

Based solely on athleticism, Darnellia was the most talented player I've coached. She had spin moves, crossovers, ball-handling skills that made the game look easy, and a shooter's touch that made her a threat anywhere on the hardwood. What made her truly remarkable, though, was her titanic teenage spirit, undefeatable in even the harshest conditions. Every lesson in this book could be taught through Darnellia's life experience off the court. She learned to own her own life when others deemed her destined to fail. She lived inch by inch, overcoming struggles on and off the court throughout her high school career. Above all, I believe Darnellia taught everyone around her life's most important lesson: *never give up.*

●

About a month before our 2000 basketball tryouts, I'd already had a dozen people tell me about a girl named Darnellia Russell who was good enough to make the varsity as a freshman. Even though the recommendations kept coming, I had my doubts. There was no way a girl I'd never heard of could be as good as they said. But considering that three gym teachers took me aside to tell me about her, I decided to check out this supposed phenom.

The first time I saw Darnellia, she was in a gym class. She stood with a basketball wedged between her right hip and wrist, her body positioned like a panther ready to pounce. Her stance was one of complete confidence, seeming to say, "This is where I belong. Don't even *try* to take my space." I approached her and said I'd heard rumors that she knew how to play basketball. She looked up with a proud, but disinterested stare. "Who are you?" she asked, though I knew she didn't care what answer I gave back. I told her I was Roosevelt's varsity basketball coach, but she brushed me off like I was a random gym rat asking for her autograph.

I told her when our tryouts would take place and about our open gym scrimmages that usually drew returning varsity players and a few underclassmen. Darnellia said she didn't know if she was going to turn out because she wasn't sure that she'd like basketball at Roosevelt. "That's really your decision, but I can understand the issue because we have an awfully good team," I retorted. She said nothing, but her look convinced me that she would prove she was worthy of being a Roosevelt varsity player.

At the time, I thought Darnellia was being a typical stand-offish teenager. I later learned Darnellia didn't plan to tryout at Roosevelt because she planned to transfer to Garfield—a South Seattle school that had won more state basketball titles than any other school in Washington. Darnellia also told Emiko Harris, a close friend since middle school, that she didn't like being around so many white people at Roosevelt, and felt comfortable at the more diverse Garfield.

She became a Roughrider only after her middle school coaches convinced Darnellia's mom that Roosevelt's academic program was a cut above Garfield's. The previous year, Roosevelt students achieved the highest cumulative scores for the Washington Assessment of Student Learning, which ranks all Seattle public schools. At the time, our daily attendance was higher than the district average, and 78 percent of Roosevelt graduates were accepted to two- and four-year colleges. While Garfield was a good school, it was no Roosevelt.

The day after our first conversation, Darnellia came to her first open gym scrimmage, and it was impossible not to take notice. Her quickness was there, and her dynamic personality included a crackling laugh—and she loved to laugh. While it may have been difficult for Darnellia to adjust to Roosevelt's mostly white environment during the school day, race didn't seem to matter between whistles. She owned the court with her basketball skill and demeanor, and during practices and games she was dead center in her comfort zone.

I watched Darnellia at the open gym for less than an hour, and then called Bryan Willison, my assistant coach. "Who's the best freshman girls basketball player at Roosevelt?" I asked. Bryan guessed wrong twice before I answered with a name he'll never forget. "Who's

Darnellia Russell?" he asked. I told Bryan he'd want to see her in person. "You won't believe how talented this girl is," I said.

Darnellia never half-assed a play, even as a freshman. She studied the opponent, and gave them slack until she had appraised all of her opponent's weaknesses. She let opponents get away with lazy crossovers two or three times, but once she exploited their weakness, the game was over.

When Darnellia dribbled the ball, she didn't think of what she was doing—the ball was an extension of her body. She watched NBA stars play, memorized their moves, and repeated them thousands of times in drills. She played against boys beginning in elementary school, and beat them by shooting layins that hit the mark 90 percent of the time. Even during water breaks she practiced dribbling moves, trying to add to her array of circus tricks.

When Bryan first watched her, he was just as impressed with her amazing quickness. But he also felt that she couldn't perform as a true team player, at least at that time. I believed that she cared about her teammates; however, she was young, and young players think the way to increase their power is to show off their skills. It became clear that it would be difficult to run an offense with her because she played like many NBA players: she'd catch the ball and drive to the hoop, ignoring any opportunities to get her teammates into the game.

We assigned Darnellia to the JV team because as a freshman we didn't think she had the ability to run an offense with her catch-and-drive mentality. Two days after tryouts, I gave my team lists to the Roosevelt athletic director, who told me he'd checked Darnellia's grades, and if she stayed the same pace, she would be ineligible for her freshman basketball season. This was a serious problem not because we might have lost her on the court, but because we might lose her in the classroom.

As soon as I left the meeting, I scheduled conferences with each of Darnellia's teachers. I was trying to come up with a plan to keep her motivated in the classroom setting, and I needed to know more.

All her teachers told me that Darnellia was a bright kid, but she missed class, didn't do her homework, and when she did show up, she showed up late.

Months before the semester ended, I found my chance right before an open gym session, and told Darnellia that unless she got serious in the classroom and her grades improved, she wouldn't be playing ball at Roosevelt. She assured me that she wouldn't miss class or be late again, and she'd do her homework, even though she hated it as all kids do. Her reassurance didn't stop me from meeting with her teachers every other week, and I asked to see her grades before the final transcripts were released. When I got them, I learned Darnellia had two Bs, a C, a D, and one E, which was a failing grade at Roosevelt. If those grades showed up on her final transcript, Darnellia's cumulative GPA would be less than a 2.0, making her ineligible for the entire basketball season.

Darnellia was currently getting an E in history, so I met with her teacher and asked him, "Who's the guy on the Roosevelt faculty who wants to make sure Darnellia Russell drops out of high school and never gets a college degree?" He looked at her grades, and realized I was referring to him. In each of our meetings, he said Darnellia had made significant improvements, and I questioned why he would fail her. He showed me her scores, which were average, but not atrocious as they had been at the start of the semester. I pointed out the improvement, but more importantly that if she failed the class, she'd be ineligible for basketball. "If she's ineligible, I guarantee she'll drop out of high school." Her teacher, who was a top-shelf guy, understood that a coach only concerned with a player's on-the-court performance wouldn't be wasting time with high school history lessons and offered to give her a D.

"No," I said. "We have to give her an extra assignment so she has another chance to improve her grade. If we just change the E to a D, it may lead her to believe that people will give her things in life. We have to make her realize that she earned it, and in the right way."

Darnellia's history teacher agreed, and assigned her a paper about World War II. Though it took her almost two weeks to write it, she earned the D that made her eligible. I was proud of her for staying on task, and I believe the experience taught her that she shouldn't wait for handouts when it comes to the game of life. If she was going to succeed, she must never give up and she must earn all of her achievements through her own hard work.

Darnellia dominated the JV with steals that looked effortless. After a tournament game in which she broke 20 points in the first half, we were even more motivated to move her up to the varsity. By the time we played that tournament game, my assistant coaches and I had already made the decision to promote her—but not because of her amazing basketball skills. If she were on the varsity, we could penalize her for missing practice, thereby creating another method of assuring she'd go to class.

Darnellia's select team coaches, my assistant Bryan Willison, and I sat down with Darnellia in early December to inform her of the promotion on the condition that she didn't miss any more practices. Bryan is much nicer than I am; consequently, he is more understanding when players miss JV practices. When a player misses a varsity practice, I make the entire team run while the tardy player watches from center court. No one wants to be the tardy girl.

Before practice that following Monday, Darnellia was hanging out in street clothes at the back of Roosevelt's gym. "I'm not going to play for the varsity," she told me. "I want to stay on the JV." I didn't give her any slack, and reiterated the conditions of our agreement. "Once you made a decision, you have to stick with what you agreed to," I said. "You can't give up." But Darnellia wanted to be with her friends on JV and didn't care what I said. "I don't give a damn what you want," I said. "You've got six minutes. And if you're not in your basketball gear and on the court, ready to practice in six minutes, then pack up your gear because you'll be done with basketball at Roosevelt."

I walked to the other end of the gym and went through the six longest minutes of outright fear I'd ever had in my life. Darnellia spent about two minutes looking disgruntled and bad-eying me before slowly making her way to the locker room. She was ready with one second remaining before practice. Her actions spoke louder than words—she made the point that I couldn't push her around, but she also showed that she was not going to give up.

In the first semester of Darnellia's sophomore year, she missed 17 classes. Earlier that year, Darnellia called Angela Nefcy to tell her she was leaving Roosevelt because she still didn't feel comfortable around so many white people. Darnellia later told me that Joyce Walker, Garfield's girls basketball coach, had been recruiting her to Garfield, playing the race card and telling Darnellia she was the missing link to a state championship Bulldog basketball team. Allegedly, Joyce also told Darnellia that she could get her a scholarship to Louisiana State University, where Joyce had been an All-American.

When the Roosevelt coaches heard Darnellia's news, my assistant Bryan Willison met with Darnellia and her mother, April, to convince her to stay. I arranged for all of Darnellia's teammates to talk to her at school the following day to tell her how much they cared about her. By the day's end, Darnellia told teammates that she would stay at Roosevelt, and I was confident that Bryan's conversation with April and Darnellia turned the tide. I also learned later that Darnellia's stepfather told her I'd always been there for her off the court, and he wasn't convinced that Joyce would do the same.

But we still had Darnellia's 17 absences to contend with. By Seattle School District guidelines, students who missed 12 or more classes in a semester fail the course. If Darnellia got all failing grades, she'd be ineligible for basketball. And if that worst-case scenario happened, I knew that from Darnellia's 16-year-old perspective, there'd be no reason for her to stay in high school.

There was an appeal process, a Roosevelt vice principal told me, but no student had ever won an appeal after missing 17 classes. I made my appeal to Darnellia's counselors, explaining that basketball was the thing that kept her in school, and we had to find a way to keep her eligible. I wasn't defending Darnellia's eligibility because she was our best player. I would have gone through the same process for the least-skilled player in our program. I fought for Darnellia because I believe sports, drama, band—all extra-curricular activities—keep kids motivated in the classroom.

Next came a group meeting with Darnellia and the Roosevelt vice principal, in which I explained with no sugar coating that if she missed another class, she would never play another high school basketball game at Roosevelt. If she decided to transfer to another school, she'd have to file a hardship appeal with WIAA, and nothing in her freshman year qualified as a hardship.

If you give up, I told her, you won't get the attention of college basketball recruiters who could want to pay your way through a university education. Any dreams of professional basketball after that would be shattered.

The vice principal told Darnellia she'd be allowed to play basketball on the condition she never missed a second semester class. We never discussed what would happen if she was sick: if she wanted what was most important to her, she would do the things that were most important for her future. Darnellia's vice principal understood that a helping hand instead of a strict adherence to detailed rules can go a long way to ensure that kids never give up.

Darnellia never missed another class during her sophomore year, including the three months following basketball season. She came to me at the end of the year, proud to say she had raised her grade point average to a 2.5.

With Darnellia in the main rotation, Roosevelt earned its fourth 4A state berth in school history behind her six-point- and three-steal-per-game average. She was impressive on the court that season, but what mattered more than any statistic was that she'd summoned the determination and strength she needed during that second semester. She didn't give up and throw in the towel. She did what she needed to do in order to get one step closer to her goals.

We knew we were an incredible team at the beginning of Darnellia's junior season. She was as much a backcourt threat as Hillary Seidel. That year, the 5-foot-9 senior averaged five steals per game during the regular season—one less than Darnellia. On our team were two 6-foot girls, Leyla Khastou and Johanna Hase; Jennie Wild, who was stronger than many guys on the Roosevelt football team; and J'nai Pich, who could score 20 points in a half on a good night.

I scheduled seven of the first eight games against teams ranked in the state's top ten, and we won them all by an average of 28 points. Darnellia's win-all mentality helped turn the Roosevelt program into a juggernaut.

A 52–51 loss to Garfield, though, served as a wake-up call, but we responded to the loss with dominating victories in a nine-game win streak. However, hostility arose between Darnellia and Hillary after Darnellia missed several Saturday morning practices. With just one family car and parents caring for three other siblings, Darnellia didn't always have a mode of transport. Based on this knowledge and knowing that Darnellia lived about 20 minutes away, I didn't penalize her as I did players who lived less than five minutes away. Because I took these factors into account, the other players thought I was giving Darnellia preferential treatment.

After a regular season game, I found Darnellia crying near the locker room. "People have been talking behind my back," she said, with tears falling on her green game jersey. I didn't think the girls were talking behind her back as much as they were wondering why she was missing practice. And that message, passed through teenagers, didn't come through in a perfect translation. Still, Darnellia didn't give up on her teammates.

The team used the Inner Circle to open up communication between Darnellia and Hillary. They realized they couldn't let off-the-court frustrations get in the way of being teammates. Once again, the Inner Circle worked its magic. Once Darnellia, Hillary, and the other teammates shared their feelings, we plowed over teams. In 11 games, we won by an average 20 points and walked through the KingCo playoffs with an aura that said, "What's the problem?"

During the hour ride to the state tournament, Darnellia stayed slumped in her seat at the back of the bus, complaining of a stomachache and back pain. Her pain persisted through the locker room pregame, and continued through halftime as we trailed 25–23. During the game we mustered up moments of intensity—we even pulled within 1 point in the third quarter—but Darnellia felt like hell, and there was nothing I could do to ignite the team. We lost our first round game 48–42, and all hope for the school's first state championship vanished.

We won the next three games to finish fifth in the state—then the highest finish in Roosevelt's history. But even with that success, Darnellia was in a foul mood, complaining about almost-overwhelming stomach and back pain in every game. When I told her she had a marvelous season as she subbed out for the last time, she didn't even acknowledge my existence as she walked to the locker room.

Two weeks after the season ended, I checked in with Darnellia's teachers and learned that she'd been missing school. I called Darnellia, but no one called me back, so I drove to her home one Saturday morning. I told her mom that Darnellia had missed about ten days of school, which she said couldn't be right because Darnellia woke and left each morning as if she were going to school. When I revealed my sources, April's face turned to a look of disgust, and seconds later, that disgust turned to anger. That past spring, the boy Darnellia had been dating since eighth grade had dropped out of high school. April knew Darnellia must be spending her school days with him.

By that point, Darnellia had missed so many classes there was no chance she'd pass any of her second semester courses. Her entire junior academic year had been ruined by her misguided decision to drop out.

April invited me back the following Saturday, and as I approached the door, Darnellia met me there. She was matter-of-fact as she told me she was four months pregnant. She'd been pregnant during the state tournament, but didn't know it at the time. Darnellia said she wasn't strong enough to make it through her classes because the pain and debilitating morning sickness made it difficult for her to even get out of bed. I sensed Darnellia was embarrassed by her short answers and uninviting eyes. Later, she told me that she felt she'd let everyone down.

I was completely calm when she gave me the news. I knew I had to be positive, and told her she must find a way to stay in school, which was most important. Basketball didn't even cross my mind. Darnellia had an obligation to herself and her expectant baby to find a way to keep going and I couldn't let her give up.

She didn't travel with the team to a tournament in San Diego the following week, and I spent the entire time brainstorming ways to get her back in the classroom. I knew she'd flunked all the second semester classes that year and considering the effort it took to keep her in school after her sophomore year, I also knew we wouldn't win an appeal that would allow her to earn credits for the classes she missed her junior year.

On advice from Roosevelt counselors, I contacted the John Marshall School, an alternative school in Seattle that offered four-week classes. Teachers at Marshall understood that a pregnancy was no reason to quit high school—it just made high school harder. I told this to Darnellia, who reenrolled there in English and math courses.

The following Monday, I approached Deborah Medler, a fellow tax professor at the University of Washington, and told her about Darnellia's condition. She volunteered to tutor Darnellia daily at her office, and above her desk put a sign in 72-point font: "Desk of Darnellia Russell, college bound." The pair started meeting the week after Roosevelt dismissed for the summer and met almost daily for three months—at least four 90-minute sessions per week. I scheduled the sessions to ensure that Darnellia knew she couldn't give up, and Deborah was one of many who felt a duty to help her keep going.

I remember one day when Deborah was out of town and I subbed in to teach Darnellia a math lesson on powers and factors. The first hypothetical I gave her was a question about the rate at which leaves accumulate. She thought for about five seconds before snapping, "How the (bleep) would I know?" I put that question away and offered another. "There are 1,024 teams in a basketball tournament," I said. "How many rounds must you have to get a champion?" She pondered for another five seconds and casually answered "ten," nailing the right answer. The questions I gave her were identical, only one discussed leaves and one discussed basketball. Darnellia never lacked intelligence; all she lacked was focus and confidence in the classroom.

I went to see the heads of Roosevelt's English and math departments to find out what Darnellia needed to do to catch up to her classmates. After hearing of her hardships, the counselors set up summer math and English courses for Darnellia, while she was still being tutored by Deborah. If she passed her summer English and math courses, it would make up for the two core classes she'd failed the previous semester. But morning sickness and pregnancy complications overwhelmed Darnellia, and she wasn't able to complete the courses.

During the fall of her senior year when she was six months pregnant, Darnellia reenrolled at Marshall. The week she applied, I met with the counselors and explained that I'd be a frequent visitor. We set weekly benchmarks in a graduation plan designed to keep her on track, and with encouragement, Darnellia's grades improved remarkably. A situation that seemed overwhelming months earlier was getting better.

When I visited at Marshall, the only time I saw Darnellia was during the final three months of her pregnancy. She told me her plan

was to give birth, be the best mommy she could, and return to her teammates, who constantly made the short walk from Roosevelt to Marshall to visit her. They all wanted her to succeed, and for the first time in her life, Darnellia's grades were above average.

Darnellia had reached a turning point since she'd learned she was pregnant, and she was now well on her way to improving herself. She had taken that "never give up" philosophy that she honed in her classes and on the basketball court, and used it to move on from this rough stint in her life. However, her "never give up" philosophy would soon be severely tested on a much different court.

During the early evening of December 1, 2002, I received an ecstatic call from Darnellia's mom, who told me that Darnellia had given birth to a baby girl, Trekayla, and that mother and daughter were doing fine. When I visited her the next morning, her bedstand was packed with cards and flowers, and the room was overflowing with teammates. The problems were still coming—how to be a mom at 18 and how to attend high school, raise a child, and maintain her improved GPA—but that hospital room was one of the happiest places I'd ever been.

In mid-January, Darnellia was back on the basketball court— only six weeks after delivering her daughter. While her mom was returning to the court, baby Trekayla was doted over by loving sitters including her father, grandmothers, and aunts. On her first day back, the team ran a fast-break drill that had eight minutes of all-out sprinting. When it was finally over, Darnellia crouched on the sidelines, gasping for air like she never had before the pregnancy. Even after giving birth, though, she went a million miles an hour in practice.

But those practices came to a devastating end after a meeting with Roosevelt's athletic director. He informed me that the Seattle School District had ruled Darnellia ineligible for the season, because she'd dropped out of school the previous semester. Since she failed her second semester courses, she didn't have the credits required to play basketball.

I found Darnellia on the baseline of the Roosevelt gym before a morning practice. I had an empty feeling, knowing I'd have to tell her that the school district declared her ineligible, and that the decision could not be appealed. Darnellia played it off like it didn't phase her a bit, which I knew meant that she was in total denial. I put my arm around her. "Sometimes adults make rules and they can't find a way to be flexible," I told her. "And because of that, you're trapped." She looked at the gym floor and asked why she'd spent so many summer hours studying with Deborah if it meant she'd still be ineligible. "Darnellia," I said, "there are many more important things in life than basketball.

"You learned very important reading and math skills that you'll use to finish high school and in college," I told her. "At this point, you have two paths. You can quit high school and go to community college, get a GED, and then play hoops at the community college level for a couple of years. Or you can come back and finish high school and get a high school degree before you go to college."

She silently packed her gear up, left the gym, and disappeared. Teammates called her; I called her. It didn't matter who left messages or how many were left. Darnellia had vanished. She told me later that she'd felt as if she'd let everyone down and she was too embarrassed to be around the team she couldn't be a part of. It was too painful for her to watch the Roughriders working their guts out and not be able to join them.

About a month later during the KingCo playoffs, Darnellia surprised everyone by coming to a winner-to-state/loser-out game against Garfield. When the Bulldogs beat us, Darnellia went into mourning, laying on the floor with her head in her hands. She hated feeling like she had given up on her teammates.

A couple weeks later, Darnellia called to tell me she was going after her high school degree. It was her stepdad, Alvin, who convinced that she'd come to the next trial. Ken argued that she was a high school student, a mother, and a girl who wanted to play basketball. The WIAA's attorney slammed Darnellia, saying that since she didn't have to pay legal fees, she could afford the bond that would keep her from fleeing jurisdiction. "Once again, the WIAA proves that they don't understand this case," Ken retorted. "I *am* charging her a fee. Someday she's going to have to do a favor for a kid, the same as what I'm doing for her." The judge smiled; I'm sure he recognized that by coming up with this special fee, Darnellia, and others, would learn a very important life lesson.

After that court hearing, the WIAA had been barred from enforcing its decision against Darnellia, pending another trial. I told the team that the WIAA would take Darnellia to trial, and if she lost that trial she'd be ineligible and we'd have to forfeit every game she played during the season. And there was no guarantee that we'd win the trial. "So, do you want Darnellia to play with you, knowing that you could have to forfeit the season, or do you want to play it safe and not let Darnellia play?" I asked.

The Inner Circle gathered and after a brief meeting, I was told they voted unanimously to play with Darnellia in defiance of the WIAA. It wouldn't matter what a governing body decided after the games were played, the girls said, because they knew they'd be true champions. And they wanted Darnellia to be seen by college recruiters who could offer her a scholarship. The players showed they would never give up on their teammate. I could not be more proud of the team. They had demonstrated an incredible amount of inner strength to support their own teammate.

Midway through the season, the WIAA appealed the injunction and forced Darnellia back to court, in an attempt to change her status to ineligible before the new trial. From my perspective, at this point it was clear that the WIAA was not simply enforcing their regulations; they were being malicious.

The entire team went to the courthouse to support Darnellia, and we were relieved to see the same judge who'd presided over our

her to get her diploma by telling her it would give her more opportunities, she said.

Darnellia didn't play that following summer, primarily because she was older than the rest of the girls and it was embarrassing for her to still be in high school. We also knew at that point that in order to play basketball as a fifth-year senior, she'd have to appeal for an eligibility hearing with the Washington Interscholastic Activities Association.

According to WIAA regulations, students under age 20 are granted four years of eligibility. A fifth year can be granted if the athlete can prove a hardship, defined as a unique set of conditions that apply solely to the athlete. The WIAA has heard hundreds of hardship appeals in this category, but does not release the facts and circumstances and rulings on these cases. I believe these disputes would be much easier to adjudicate if the WIAA would release this important information.

I knew Darnellia longed to play, so I stepped in to assist her with an appeal. I met with the Roosevelt athletic director, and we completed the required paperwork so Darnellia would get the first available hearing in September. All she had to do was demonstrate a hardship in order to be deemed eligible, and all the coaches thought it was a slam dunk. The reason she missed so much school was due to the morning sickness caused by her pregnancy, which made it too painful for her to get out of bed. She had a daughter at 18, and even after she was denied eligibility by the Seattle School District, she returned to complete her classes, and she raised her cumulative GPA. In my mind, she had turned her hardship into a true success story, and she deserved a fifth year of play.

I accompanied Darnellia and her mom to the hearing at the WIAA office. Darnellia cried as she described the devastating uncertainty that came with a teenage pregnancy. She gave details of her debilitating morning sickness and apologized directly to me for letting the Roosevelt program down. Darnellia also told the WIAA officials how she loved the daughter she was raising while attending classes. As I listened to her speech, I felt that no thinking person could deny that a difficult pregnancy was a hardship.

Two days later, the WIAA sent a fax denying Darnellia's appeal. I was shocked. I realized that either Darnellia's situation was, in fact, not really a hardship, or those three male WIAA officials valued cut-and-dried rules over giving kids who deserve it a second chance to succeed.

I found Darnellia in a hallway after a class at Marshall and when I gave her the bad news, she stared at me for what seemed like an hour. "We're not done," I told her. "This isn't the end. We're going to go all the way to court to appeal this if we have to." Still, she was too stunned to speak.

A Roosevelt parent told me of attorney Ken Luce, who had represented athletes against the arbitrary rulings of the WIAA. I called him and explained the facts of Darnellia's case. "Is she a good kid?" he asked. "She's a great kid," I told him. "And I have a moral duty to help her graduate from college. I'm not going to give up on her."

He told me the lawsuit would cost approximately $25,000 with legal fees and court costs, and I explained there was no way Darnellia could raise that kind of money because she came from one of the poorest neighborhoods in Seattle. "You're a lawyer aren't you, Resler?" I told him I was. "Lawyers usually listen a little better than you did," Ken said. "I said it was going to cost $25,000. I didn't say I was going to charge her that. Bring her down to my office."

Darnellia, her mother, and I met Ken at his office three days later. He explained how much each step of the lawsuit would cost and said he absolutely needed to be paid for the work. As Ken insisted on a fee, April's hands clenched with fear. "So here's my legal fee," he said, staring at Darnellia. "Someday you will have to do a favor for somebody like I'm doing for you." Ken didn't want her to give up.

We discussed the facts of the case and when we were finished, Ken told me it was as good a set of facts as he'd ever had when fighting the WIAA. And things were looking good. At that point, his record was 33–1.

That fall, a male representative from the WIAA heard our t. appeal. Ken explained that Darnellia didn't plan to get pregnan, didn't know she was pregnant, and missed school only when she was sick, as any kid would have. Ken argued that if a student was sick and missed too many days of school, that case would be a hardship. If a student had missed school because of a car wreck, that would be considered a hardship. A student who couldn't play because of an emotionally degrading coach would be granted a reprieve due to hardship, Ken argued. In each of his hardship examples, a student would be granted a fifth year of athletic eligibility. Darnellia's case, as Ken demonstrated, was a hardship. "If you think it's not the same," he said, "then your decision violates her constitutional rights because in this situation, males don't get punished for having a child, but females do." If Darnellia was declared ineligible, she would not receive equal protection under the law, which is required by the constitution.

The WIAA still ruled her ineligible, but that time, they added to their defense: she made her own choices. The WIAA felt Darnellia had caused her own hardship by getting pregnant and choosing to have her baby.

Ken and his law partner docketed a pretrial hearing so they could get an injunction that would prevent the WIAA from enforcing its decision against Darnellia. The judge assigned to the case had spent years as a juvenile court judge, and I could imagine the kind of hardships he'd seen. In district court, parties were allowed to excuse one judge with a preemptive strike. Given the judge's background, I don't know why the WIAA didn't excuse him. It seems as though they didn't care or didn't do their homework.

The judge didn't even get to hear the debate of whether Darnellia's situation was a hardship. He ruled that the WIAA's decision was unconstitutional because it could only be enforced upon women.

We were thrilled with the judge's ruling, but just when we thought the WIAA couldn't get any more insulting, their attorney requested that Darnellia be required to file a bond that guaranteed first hearing. The WIAA argued that if Darnellia was allowed to play, other girls might choose to get pregnant to obtain a fifth year of athletic eligibility. The judge looked out at the team and said, "I don't think any of Darnellia's teammates are thinking, 'I'm going to get pregnant so I can go to a fifth year of high school.'" The court upheld the injunction, and to no one's surprise, the WIAA said they would take the case to court when the season was over.

Darnellia was thrilled coming out of the court room because she knew she could finish the season, and I was thrilled knowing she had even more motivation to stay in school. I got a call from Alvin, Darnellia's stepdad, later that afternoon. He thanked me for standing up for Darnellia, and said she had learned the most important lesson there is to know when it comes to life. We nearly spoke simultaneously: "Never give up."

That season, Darnellia was phenomenal, averaging 14.3 points per game. With her strong game supporting an already strong team, we entered the KingCo 4A tournament with a seven-game win streak. We advanced to the league championship against Garfield, but lost in overtime after the Bulldogs forged a late-game surge. In the postgame locker room, Darnellia promised her teammates that they'd avenge the loss by beating the Bulldogs at the state tournament. I didn't tell her that it was highly unlikely we'd face Garfield again that season, since a rematch could happen only if both teams won three straight state tournament games. And at that point, we hadn't even secured a state berth. But the next night, Darnellia came through on the first part of her promise as the emotional leader in a 42–41 loserout game that gave us the league's state tournament berth.

We crushed our first state opponent by 23 points and earned a 59–50 win in the quarterfinals behind Darnellia's 14 points. Darnellia and her teammates were so confident they would beat Snohomish, our semifinal opponent, that they wanted to watch

Garfield's semifinal game so they could scout out their strategies and weak spots before the championship. Throughout Garfield's semifinal game, the Roughriders cheered the Bulldogs because they wanted their revenge in the final. The season wouldn't be complete, Darnellia said, until we defeated Garfield.

After Roosevelt beat Snohomish and advanced to Saturday's state final for the first time in school history, Ward Serrill approached Garfield coach Joyce Walker and noted how lucky it was that Roosevelt would be playing Garfield in the championship. Joyce responded, "Maybe for you it is." After hearing about that, I made sure every girl heard that comment multiple times before the championship game tip-off. At our pre-game locker room meeting, I asked the team why Joyce was worried. Darnellia was the first to answer. "We're the better team," she said. "And we won't give up."

Given the Inner Circle's decision earlier in the season to play in defiance of the WIAA's ruling even though it might cost us the season if we lost the battle in court, I felt I had a moral duty to play each girl in the state championship game. They supported Darnellia; I was going to support them. If we lost the game it would be my fault.

In the locker room before the championship game, every girl knew we'd go home with the championship trophy. Darnellia and Maggie Torrance sat side by side chattering about game strategy with body language that showed they would not have been afraid to take on the WNBA all-star team. The team never gave up during the season, and Darnellia told the Roughriders they wouldn't this time, either.

But someone forgot to inform Garfield that the state championship was ours to win, and they exploded to a 9–0 lead. We were about to call time-out when Maggie nailed a three from the right corner that set our team on fire. Then Darnellia went to work. She scored a pair of layins during our run that ended the first quarter tied at 11. In the final 30 seconds of the second quarter, Darnellia launched a 3-pointer from the left corner. It went in with 17.6 seconds remaining and our team erupted—we knew we were in control. We rallied from a 9–0 deficit with a 20–5 run orchestrated by Darnellia, who led all first-half scorers with 13 points.

The game had eight lead changes, seven ties, and with 3:09 remaining, Darnellia's free throw gave us a 51–50 lead. With 1:04 left and the Roughriders clinging to a 53–52 lead, Garfield missed a layin and Darnellia forced a jump ball, which gave us possession. Senior Breianna Gaines made a foul shot with 36 seconds remaining to give us a 2-point lead. But against the Bulldogs, a 2-point lead wasn't enough to make us feel comfortable. We were 5.6 seconds away from a title when Garfield went to the line for two free throws. The Bulldogs didn't score either shot, and with 4.2 seconds Breianna was fouled under the Bulldog basket.

The moment was saturated with anxiety, but Darnellia wasn't phased. The television broadcast shows her calmly conversing as she walked down court with Breianna, telling her that we were in control and were going to win. But Breianna missed her foul shot, and the rebound went towards 6-foot-2 Garfield center Jamila Bates. If Garfield's potent offense gained possession, they'd be a dangerous threat.

True to form, Darnellia didn't give up against her opponents. Despite her small 5-foot-6 frame, she pulled away from two oversized Garfield players and snagged the crucial rebound, forcing Garfield to foul her with 1.9 seconds remaining.

Her free throw was the final point in the school's first state championship. Afterward the girls jumped on each other, jumped on the floor, hugged each other, hugged the other team, and screamed their brains out. Darnellia gave me one of the best hugs I've ever felt. "You are awesome," I said, through her tears of joy. "You should be so proud of yourself."

I could write an entire book just about that game and the hundreds of touching moments that allowed us to be champions. But when people ask me to explain in a sentence how we won the championship, there's only one answer: Darnellia inspired her teammates. She had overcome more obstacles in two years than many people face in a lifetime. And the team didn't quit because Darnellia proved to them why they shouldn't. In that state championship game, and in life, she never, ever gave up.

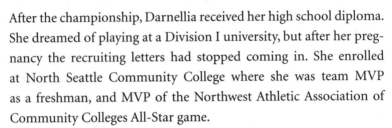

After the championship, Darnellia received her high school diploma. She dreamed of playing at a Division I university, but after her pregnancy the recruiting letters had stopped coming in. She enrolled at North Seattle Community College where she was team MVP as a freshman, and MVP of the Northwest Athletic Association of Community Colleges All-Star game.

She didn't get a scholarship because her grades weren't stellar during her first year at North Seattle, and she didn't convince college coaches that she wasn't going to fail. Even all-state players have a hard time securing offers from top schools. Colleges are not going to waste money on somebody who isn't going to succeed academically, and initially, Darnellia didn't prove to them that she would succeed.

During her first year of college, Darnellia missed four math tests and was told she'd be ineligible for her sophomore season if she didn't take those tests. Darnellia realized that she might not be able to play basketball, so she studied with my middle daughter, Alexa, who had graduated with a math degree from the University of Washington. Alexa worked with Darnellia for ten days to prepare her for the four makeup tests. When Darnellia checked her scores, she received a 94 percent, 96, 98, and 94. She may have not known how to study, but she was certainly smart enough to succeed.

Sure there were days when I worried about Darnellia at North Seattle. Her situation wasn't easy—trying to continue her education and play the game she lived for, while being a dedicated mother of an active toddler. But I know how smart Darnellia is, and I know that she taught her teammates to never give up.

It would have been easy to give up on Darnellia when her poor grades made her ineligible in high school. It would have been understandable if she didn't come back to the team she thought she let down by getting pregnant. Many kids wouldn't have the endurance to keep fighting after the WIAA's malicious attempts to reject her hardship appeal. But Darnellia Russell isn't like many kids. She's unlike anyone I've ever met. And I, and everyone else lucky enough to have met her, learned from Darnellia what I believe is life's most important lesson.

CHAPTER ELEVEN

Conclusion

Coach Bill Resler (Photograph by Casey McNerthney)

Always Have Fun
in All Ways

People ask me why it is I continue to coach high school girls basketball despite the fact that my daughters are grown and that the job takes up a considerable amount of time. It certainly isn't for the money. I could make more money mowing lawns in a summer than I do as a high school girls basketball coach. If a person coaches high school girls basketball for money or fame, they're insane. Good coaches devote so many hours of their lives solely because they love the players they teach. They know that the true payoff doesn't come from a winning on-court feat—it comes years after the girls graduate from high school, when I see them walking tall and strong and I know they gained much of their confidence through the life lessons they learned on the court. Without a doubt, I coach for the love of the game, but I also coach because it gives me the opportunity to pass on the important lessons I've learned to all of the wonderful students under my watch.

Just as I'm not involved in coaching for the money, I didn't write this book because I want more people to recognize me. I wrote this book because I want people to recognize their own power through the life lessons I share within these pages. Whether it's learning to never give up or the importance of sacrifice for the good of a team, these lessons go beyond the basketball court and are just as important in the game of life.

I know that in order for my players to get the most out of their basketball seasons, they must be able to own their own turf—and this translates to their lives off the court, too. In Roughrider land, the basketball key is our home. We will share our home with teammates, but not with the opponents. When an opponent flashes through the key, we will smash them. We run a drill called "Smash the Flash," which teaches the girls that no one is allowed in our key and any opponent who does so will get knocked to the hardwood. As the girls often say, "Not in our kitchen." Owning the actual basketball court is important, but it represents just one part of a player's turf. When players learn to work with teammates while controlling their turf, they're practicing skills that will help them deal with future life experiences.

When kids are young, their parents are their primary educators. Most parents understand that as their little ones grow up, they need to be given more and more space as they edge towards independence. Parents need to understand that high school sports provide an environment where their kids can learn to assert themselves and grow as individuals. But in order for that to happen, young athletes must be allowed to take the helm themselves, and navigate unexplored waters using their own steering mechanisms, without parental involvement.

Whenever I talk with former players about what they've accomplished after graduating from Roosevelt, I get the same feeling that comes watching my team secure a victory in the final seconds of a game. Alaina Forbes enrolled at Washington State University in 2003, and when she told me she was studying for her Ph.D. in chemistry, I was as thrilled as I'd be if she were my own daughter. After graduating in 1999, Lindsey Wilson earned an athletic scholarship to Iowa State University where she became a second-team All-American, and later played professionally in Greece and Turkey. When Lindsey heard Roosevelt was in the 2004 state championship, she sent me an e-mail that I read to the team.

"I'm 22 years old, been out of high school almost five years now," Lindsey wrote. "I've played all over the country and all over the world. I've played in big games, played on TV in front of thousands of people. Yet, when I walk into the Roosevelt gym, my heart still swells with emotion. I hope the girls know how good they have it, for you [Coach Resler] and I both know they will go out into the world and do their thing, but they'll always remember this year, this game, this moment when their whole world is wrapped up in one night."

By now, you've read all about the essential life lessons that I teach to my students. However, there is one guiding principle that pushes my life and that drives all of these lessons: *always have fun in all ways.* Every other teaching standard and life lesson flows from this key philosophy. As I discussed in Chapter 8, I believe that if your life isn't fun, you should change it. Every person views fun in their own way, but not everyone pursues it as their paramount principle. It's unlikely that everyone is comfortable with placing "always have fun" at the top of their life-goals list, but for me, there is no other course. For those of you who disagree, take a moment to consider that placing fun on the highest pedestal can make it easier to be in the moment, even when you're facing a truly difficult and challenging situation.

All of the lessons I've taught the Roughriders through the years are important. But I feel that employing a teaching style that utilizes fun aspects when possible is incredibly helpful, especially when dealing with confidence boosting. Much of my coaching comes sprinkled with wicked sarcasm and impish pranks. I believe that to be effective, I must create an aura of unpredictability, so during practice I spout out crazy comments at random times. I do this for two reasons: first, to keep them alert, and most important, to remind them that we must always have fun in all ways.

For example, during one practice I told junior Mackenzie Argens, "That's the third worst pass I have ever seen in basketball." Biting the lure, she responded, "At least there are two worse than mine." I struck, "True, the two passes you threw yesterday were much worse." Mackenzie laughed as did the senior players because that is a little wordplay I save for juniors, and those seniors had already been to that dance. I was able to make it clear that Mackenzie had to work on her passing, but brought the message home with a punchline. Though she was criticized, she had a good laugh in the process.

Julia Koerner, one of the quickest guards in Roosevelt history, was guarding Grace Cappleman, a 6-foot-2 freshman post. Grace fooled her on a backdoor cut, got the pass, and banked in a layin. Julia exclaimed, "She's so tall." I responded with a grin, "And she's apparently quicker too!" One minute later the same matchup occurred. Julia guarded Grace so tightly that it seemed that she was part of her jersey. Grace never had a chance to touch the ball, let alone score. Julia strolled by me and whispered, "Quicker, my ass." I smiled. It is all about motivation. A coach or teacher must constantly search for opportunities to motivate. If you keep your eyes alert, the chances abound. Because motivation is such a touchstone for me, I suspect I don't miss many golden opportunities.

The most difficult part of teaching life lessons is finding the right vehicle to help teenagers understand them. Sometimes, a conversation with a player will spark her interest about a particular lesson. In other instances, a tête-à-tête with a teenager will be completely disregarded as pointless blather pouring out of an aging coach. Recognizing those perfect moments requires constant guesswork, and there aren't that many golden opportunities, so I always capitalize whenever one of these golden moments drops in my lap. For me, a great opportunity came with Korleona Davico, a player who "joined" our team at the beginning of the 2001–02 season. The case could be made that Davico was the most important player in all my years at Roosevelt.

That season, we opened it up against Kamiakin on their home court. We were milling around waiting for the first tip-off of the season, when I noticed a readerboard on the gym wall. "Welcome Roughriders," it read, with the jersey numbers of each player and her last name. The fourth line read "9 - K. Davico," a name I'd never heard of. Even more confusing, we didn't have a number nine jersey and there wasn't a student at Roosevelt with that name. Rather than waste time by complaining to whoever ran the readerboard, I saw this as a perfect opportunity for fun and motivation.

Standing in the midcourt circle I yelled to the hoard of Roosevelt girls gossiping in the bleachers, "Davico! Come over here!" A few of them looked up at me, wondered what in the world I was talking about, then went back to ignoring me. A few minutes later, I pressed on, "Davico, get over here!" Again, I got looks like I was nuts, and they returned to their conversations.

About ten minutes later, I walked to the edge of the bleachers, stood over them, and again asked the Roughriders if anyone knew where Davico was. "Who the (bleep) is Davico?" Darnellia Russell asked, vocalizing the players' looks of confusion.

I locked eyes with her and spoke in a dead serious tone, "That's real good, Darnellia. We're about to have the first game of the season and you don't even know your teammates." The other girls picked up on my tone and all paid attention after the first sentence of my rant. "Knowing and respecting your teammates is the most essential ingredient to having a great team. I can't believe you don't care one bit about Davico. You better figure out who your team is and you better do it now," I spat out, with arms flapping and a Bobby Knight complexion. I wheeled on my heels and stormed out of the gym. Over my shoulder I heard Darnellia say, "He's so stupid."

I was standing in the foyer about 30 minutes later when senior Jennie Wild approached and slung her arm over my shoulder. "Bill, I can't believe you thought that Davico thing was funny," she said. "You're such a dork." She had seen the readerboard and figured out the prank.

As the girls took their seats in the pre-game locker room, I asked if everyone was present. Jennie said, "Davico isn't here yet." This launched the girls into a cacophony of put-downs of their imaginary teammate. That wasn't just music to my ears—it was a full-on symphony. At the end of my pre-game pep talk, I told the girls that it would be a tough game, and we would have to work incredibly hard. When I finished my comments, I said, "Let's go out and win this game for Davico." We put our hands together and yelled "*Davico!*" as we broke from our huddle. When the final buzzer put a stop to our all-out aggression, Roosevelt had dominated Kamiakin 64–28. My plan had worked, and I'd set in motion an insider joke that didn't end with our victory over Kamiakin.

Throughout that season, I motivated the players with references to Davico. When we played a Canadian team, I told them it was a grudge match. "We hate these Canadians," I said, "because they were responsible for Davico's deportation out of Canada." When we played Garfield, we had it out for them because, as the story goes, actual bulldogs mauled Davico and put her on the disabled list. This imaginary player's story could be molded in any situation to make tense game situations fun, and each new story provided fresh motivation to get out there and win one for poor Davico.

Midway through the season we beat Woodinville High 62–30. After the game, a reporter from the *Eastside Journal* asked me why Roosevelt was so consistently dominant. "It was a defensive masterpiece," I said. "They just went out there and flew around." I don't like to lie to anyone, especially reporters, but that day, I thought I was justified in playing a harmless prank that would crack up my players. I told the reporter about our fallen teammate, the mysterious Davico, and that the players wanted to honor her with a win. "The Roughriders dedicated the game to Korleona Davico, who suffered a year-ending knee injury earlier in the week," wrote the reporter, who added my quote that, "The girls really wanted to win this one for her."

Before a playoff game, I wrote a letter from Davico to the team. In it, Korleona Davico took credit for everything that went well that season—the close wins, the team camaraderie. "Without me," the letter said, "this team wouldn't be squat."

I'm sure we would have played very well without Davico that year, but in a way, that letter was accurate. Without the fun and inspiration provided by our imaginary player, we wouldn't have had nearly as many positive, fun moments. And those moments helped emphasize lessons that are far more important than our team record.

Whenever we go to state, I create inspirational T-shirts for each of the girls. That season, on the sleeve was the word "Davico." At the state tournament, nearly all of the local newspapers covering our games ran articles mentioning Davico. Opposing coaches would ask me if I was going to put my imaginary player in the game. To this day June Daugherty, the extraordinary coach of the Washington Huskies, asks me to tell her fellow coaches the Davico story.

When I first saw the name "Davico" on the readerboard, I pounced on the opportunity to have fun. When the girls caught on to the fun factor of their new teammate, they took the ball and ran with it. So, I kept Davico around because her fictional scenarios allowed me to teach lessons before each game, but more importantly the lessons came packaged in fun.

This book is brought together by basketball, but it's not about the game. Davico's story and each of the girls I've written about convey life lessons packaged in fun that I believe are sure-fire ways to help young athletes and others become better people.

As I wrote this book, I reflected on my eight seasons as Roosevelt's coach and considered all that I've accomplished, which is something I rarely do. I honestly don't care about Roosevelt's win-loss record or how many championships we've won. More than any statistic, I care about the lessons my players learn from the experience, and how they will utilize those lessons decades after the final buzzer of their basketball careers. What I value most is knowing that I've made a positive impact on the lives of many teenagers. My players, and the moments they created, have brought me more fun that I can fit into words. And I hope you had fun reading this book.

Acknowledgments

This book is a reflection of my heartfelt desire to chase down exuberant laughter regularly. I believe that we are on this planet to have fun while trying not to hurt anyone. There are several people who made this book possible. The joy given to me by my three daughters—Jessica, Alexa, and Vanessa—allowed me to proceed through life with as much frivolity as possible. If *The Heart of the Game* was not created, there would be no book. Thank you Ward Serrill for entering my life and helping me carry on with my adventures.

I could write an entire book about my parents, Joseph Howard and Cora Jean Resler, and my sister, Judi, who were the first to demonstrate the lessons I teach. My wife, Sherry Resler, and stepdaughter, Miranda, can't be thanked enough for the love and support they've given me. Gerry Wallace, my friend and mentor at New York University, is the reason I am a teacher, and professor Charlie Lyon taught me more than any other that life should be fun. We are truly two peas from the same pod. Thanks also go to my nieces and nephew—Pam, Litsa, and Jarrod—and University of Washington colleagues Julius Roller and Durwood Alkire for their years of support.

Casey McNerthney is the direct reason there is a book. I call him "the boot," as he was the boot in my tail that kept me working. His friendship, sense of humor, and eagerness to do the right thing pushed me to accomplish this project.

From the first day with Sasquatch Books, every person involved demonstrated that, while writing this book might be work, we were going to have loads of fun in the process, and we did because of them. Editorial director Gary Luke, marketing coordinator Courtney

Payne, and publicist Austin Walters kept us looking forward to office visits. Designer Bob Suh couldn't have created a better cover or been more fun to hang out with during the book's creation. Copy editor Ellen Dendy and proofreader Shari Miranda were extremely thorough and enjoyable to work with. More than any other, this book was made possible by the kind heart and unwavering patience of editor Terence Maikels. He was the veteran coach helping two rookies, and the success of this book is a credit to his talent.

The incredible family I've become associated with at the Duchess Bar and Social Club has always kept my spirits soaring. A mighty big thank you goes to Boyd Hansen for creating our Duchess family. I have so many friends and people I am friendly with, and they should know how much they improve my days.

There would be no book without Aileen McManus, who, as the former head coach of the Roughriders, hired me to be her assistant. I learned the basics about coaching from her; however, it was her total devotion to sportsmanship and humanity that became the touchstones of my approach to coaching.

Steve Rice, my favorite professor and friend, introduced me to Ward Serrill and also introduced me to the intricacies of the joys of music. I would not be the person I am today without the friendship of Trila Bumstead. And though he died nearly 20 years ago, my thoughts often drift to my dearest friend, Tom Cropley.

—*Bill Resler*

This book would not be possible without John Harris, a Western Washington University journalism professor who inspired a misguided marketing student. Patrick Sullivan, managing editor of the *Port Townsend and Jefferson County Leader*, is a teacher and friend who gave me a chance when I was too young to realize my obvious mistakes. Without a job opportunity from Nick Rousso, sports editor at the *Seattle Post-Intelligencer*, I would still be stuck making double-tall, no-foam lattés at 5 a.m. wondering "What if . . ." I couldn't dream of a better boss than Nick, or *P-I* sports editor Ron Matthews, who is a shoo-in for the All-Time Coolest People List. The same goes for *P-I* editor Bill Hayes. Thanks also go to *P-I* photographer Gilbert Arias for capturing the spirit of Molly Boyd, and to *P-I* publisher Roger Oglesby for letting us reprint it.

Thanks to Bill Resler, a friend who taught me more than I can thank him for. And because of Ward Serrill's heart, millions more hearts have been inspired. Though Nicole Brodeur knows how cool she is, I'll keep reminding her as long as Bruce Springsteen wears Levi's. Whenever my mood made Oscar the Grouch look like a lightweight, Brian Mara, Pat Moynihan, and Nicole Newman were the friends who made me remember that life should be fun. And I have a wonderful life because they are in it.

My uncle, Joe McNerthney, helped me through the writing process and every other important stage of life. My parents, Pat and Wendy McNerthney, started teaching me this book's lessons years before I could write my own name. Every time someone compliments me, I appreciate it but know that all I'm doing is following their models. I'd be truly lucky to someday be as good at parenting as they have been.

—*Casey McNerthney*

About the Authors

Bill Resler has been head coach of the Roosevelt High Roughriders girls basketball team since the 1998–99 season, and inspired millions with his lessons of all-out aggression in the award-winning documentary *The Heart of the Game*. In his inaugural season as head coach, Resler led the Roughriders to their first Class 4A state tournament berth in 18 years and was named coach of the year by *The Seattle Times*. Since then, the Roughriders have won four league titles and have participated in the state tournament five times, winning the state title in 2004.

After an adventurous undergraduate experience at Washington State University, Resler earned a law degree from the University of Washington in 1971. He received his LL.M. in taxation in 1972 from New York University School of Law, where he went on to be the youngest faculty member following his graduation. He began teaching tax at the University of Washington School of Business in 1978, became director of the Masters of Professional Accounting (Taxation) program in 1992, and was the accounting Undergraduate Professor of the Year in 2006.

A Seattle native, Resler is the proud father of three daughters.

Casey McNerthney is a sports correspondent for the *Seattle Post-Intelligencer*. A graduate of Western Washington University, he lives in Seattle.

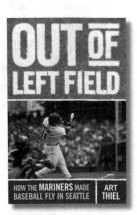